PABLO
PICASSO

BOOKS BY RICHARD B. LYTTLE

PEOPLE OF THE DAWN
Early Man in the Americas

WAVES ACROSS THE PAST
Adventures in Underwater Archaeology

THE GAMES THEY PLAYED
Sports in History

THE GOLDEN PATH
The Lure of Gold through History

LAND BEYOND THE RIVER
Europe in the Age of Migration

IL DUCE
The Rise and Fall of Benito Mussolini

PABLO PICASSO
The Man and the Image

In the 1932 **Girl Before a Mirror,** *64″ × 51¼″, Picasso's technique of showing both frontal and profile views of a face is used to excellent advantage. Here the mirror image also allows him to play with another level of reality.*

PABLO PICASSO

THE MAN
AND
THE IMAGE

RICHARD B. LYTTLE

Atheneum   1989   New York

This book is for Dean Snodgrass and Lonicera Lyttle

Atheneum
Macmillan Publishing Company
866 Third Avenue, New York, NY 10022
Collier Macmillan Canada, Inc.
First Edition
Printed in the United States of America

Designed by Trish Parcell Watts

10 9 8 7 6 5 4 3 2 1

Library of Congress Cataloging-in-Publication Data
Lyttle, Richard B.
Pablo Picasso:the man and the image.
Bibliography: p.
1. Picasso, Pablo, 1881–1973. 2. Artists—France
—Biography. I. Title.
N6853.P5L98   1989   709.2   [B]   89–6561
ISBN 0–689–31393–4

Although several friends gave much-needed help and encouragement throughout this project, special thanks are due Dr. George H. Rodetis, professor of Art History at Sonoma State University, who read the finished manuscript and made several valuable suggestions.

CONTENTS

	The Man and the Image	ix
1.	Child of Spain	1
2.	Barcelona	12
3.	The Dropout	21
4.	The Blue Period	30
5.	The Rose Period	42
6.	The Steins	53
7.	Cubism	62
8.	Ma Jolie	73
9.	World War	82
10.	Olga Khoklova	93
11.	Married Life	103
12.	Marie-Thérèse	111

13. Guernica   126
14. World War II   139
15. Liberation   152
16. Life with Françoise   162
17. Farewell to Paris   173
18. The Hectic Life   187
19. Life with Jacqueline   198
20. Big Works   208
21. Married Again   219
22. The Final Years   230
    Bibliography   238
    Index   240

THE MAN AND THE IMAGE

This is the story of an artistic genius who lived through some of the most turbulent times the world has known. Pablo Picasso not only survived to a proud age, but he also produced a huge body of work, so huge that it is difficult to come to terms with it. Even those who know his work well cannot claim to understand it fully.

His personal life, subject to intense public scrutiny, was not always exemplary, but we cannot consider his art apart from his life. Few artists have responded so faithfully and honestly to their day-to-day experiences and passions. The man and the image really are one.

Because production costs make it impossible to do justice to his work in one book, I strongly recommend that you read this with companion volumes that have many reproductions of his paintings and prints, and photos of his sculpture. Your library should have a good selection.

Also, be prepared to stretch your artistic judgment. It is a woeful simplification to "like" or "dislike" Picasso's art. He was too complex, too diverse to be weighed so subjectively. Your first goal should be to understand one of our century's most influential men. Then you can form your own assessment of his work. This book will help you begin.

1

CHILD OF SPAIN

He was born late in the evening of October 25, 1881, in a large apartment house in the poor district of Málaga, an old town on the southern coast of Spain. His father, Don José Ruiz Blasco, an art teacher, and his mother, Doña María Picasso y Lopez, had been married for a year. He was thirty-one. She was twenty-six. Their first child barely survived birth.

It was later said that the attending doctor, Salvador Ruiz Blasco, the father's brother, blew cigar smoke in the baby's face to start him gasping. In this way, according to legend, Pablo Picasso drew his first breath.

The situation was actually quite serious. The midwife, thinking the baby had been born dead, put him aside to give all her attention to the mother. In an act of desperation, the doctor got the boy breathing, not with cigar smoke but rather with a firm smack on the behind.

The boy's dark eyes widened, his squarish face reddened, and his mouth opened with a lusty wail. A long and eventful life had begun.

On November 10, barely more than two weeks after the ordeal, mother and child had recovered enough for the rite of baptism. Because this baptism was for the the first male heir of his generation, it was an especially festive event. Friends and relatives flocked to Santiago el Mayor, the parish church, to hear the baby christened Pablo Diego José Francisco de Paula Juan Nepomuceno Cipriano de la Santissima Trinidad María de los Romedios Alarcón y Herrera Ruiz-Picasso. Such long names were common, for it was the tradition in Spain to honor all relatives at a baptism. "Pablo" came from a wealthy uncle who had recently died. "Ruiz-Picasso," through another tradition, combined the father's and mother's family names.

His parents were far from wealthy, but the family ties were plentiful.

Don José was the ninth of eleven brothers and sisters. Salvador, the doctor, not only took care of the family's medical needs, but he also offered to assist with the education of the children. Many other friends and relatives were concerned with Pablo's well-being. Two unmarried aunts and a grandmother shared the family apartment. They helped care for Pablo and instruct him in the first principles of life. Pablo's godfather was a lawyer who acted as family adviser on legal and business matters.

Don José needed help. Moody, sad, and thoughtful, he sometimes seemed to be a tragic figure unable to face reality, let alone responsibility. He was not a typical Spaniard. He did not even look like one. Tall, with sharp features and reddish hair and beard, he had been nicknamed "the Englishman." Pablo's mother, on the other hand, was unmistakably

Spanish, with her fierce pride, quick changes of temper, jet black hair, and dark, flashing eyes.

In looks Pablo took after his mother. He had a short, compact build. His dark, mobile eyes, exactly like his mother's, dominated his squarish face. The eyes, intensely passionate at one moment, could be deeply thoughtful the next. From his father, Pablo inherited a full range of moods: stubborn or sullen one moment, happy or angry the next. Also, he guarded his independence with fierce determination.

Don José had known tragedy. His life had been changed by the early death of an older brother, Pablo Ruiz Blasco. A highly placed, wealthy clergyman, the brother had encouraged José to become a painter and had paid for his instruction. In conservative Spain, painting as a career was looked on with suspicion. Most painters were seen as ne'er-do-wells, bohemian types who did not attend church regularly. As long as Don José had Pablo's support, however, no one looked down on him. But in 1878, the sudden death of Pablo and the loss of his backing brought a change in status. Two unmarried sisters, once Uncle Pablo's responsibility, now became Don José's. And he wanted the further responsibility of marriage for himself.

Don José had to go to work, and the only job available for a man of his training was teaching at the San Telmo School of Arts and Crafts. Later, to earn extra money, he worked as curator for the city's art museum. The women in the household supplemented Don José's salary by sewing uniforms for city workers. Occasionally, but only occasionally, Don José sold a painting.

One of young Pablo's most vivid early memories was the arrival of his sister Lola. She was born on Christmas night, 1884, not long after a sharp earthquake jolted Málaga. Don José had rushed his family to the home of Antonio Muñoz Degrain, a friend and fellow painter, who lived on the ground floor. There Lola was born. Pablo remembered that his

3

mother fled to Degrain's house wearing a handkerchief over her head. His father wore a huge cloak that he wrapped around Pablo so that only the boy's head was exposed.

Lola's birth, however, may not have been his earliest memory. Pablo claimed that he could remember his first steps, taken while pushing a large cookie tin across the floor of the apartment.

Málaga in the 1880s was a happy place in which to grow up. Its ruins of a Phoenician fortress more than two thousand years old could set a boy dreaming of imaginary battles and conquests. Built upon the ruins were two Moorish castles that were more than a thousand years old. The castles stood on the hillside above town and gave a clear view across the Strait of Gibraltar to the snowcapped Ajax Mountains of Northern Africa.

Don José's paintings, generally known at the time as "dining-room pictures," had little to do with his surroundings. He specialized in still-life scenes that usually featured colorful blooms or birds and animals. He tried to make everything look real, real enough to touch.

Pablo spent hours watching his father paint. And at a very early age, he wanted to make his own pictures. His parents encouraged him. His mother recalled that *lápiz*, Spanish for pencil, was Pablo's first word. Actually, he began drawing long before he could speak. Spirals were one of his favorite shapes, perhaps because they resembled Spanish sugar cakes.

Later Pablo accompanied his father to the city museum where Don José had set up a small studio. Pablo watched the pictures take shape on the canvases.

Although Don José had a limited range, he was not afraid to experiment. In an effort to solve complex compositions, he might make painted cutouts of pigeons and shift them around on his canvas until their positions suited him. Another experiment was not so successful. For this he painted a plaster cast of a Madonna to create what Pablo remem-

4

bered as an extremely ugly statue. But Don José's devotion to realism, combined with the courage to experiment, was not a bad legacy to pass on to his talented son.

When friends came by the studio, Pablo would listen for hours as they discussed the world of art. Señor Degrain, the man who had sheltered Don José and his family at the time of the earthquake, had been to Paris and had adopted some of the techniques of the impressionists, whose use of color and light were still considered quite daring in conservative Spain. To Pablo, it was all fascinating.

And then there were the bullfights. Don José was a real fan, and he instilled a lifelong love for the bullring in his son. Pablo's happiest memories of his father centered on Sundays, the days of the bullfights. The bullring was on the hillside above town, not far from the Moorish castles. It was easy to walk to the ring from their home on the Plaza de la Merced.

For a Spaniard, the bullfight is a ritual of life and death. It is the conquest over chaos—represented by the bull—by civilization—represented by the horsemen and the skillful toreador. The bull is seen as a brute driven by rage and instinct. The toreador is a priest, an athlete, and an artist. Sundays were the best days of Pablo's young life.

School was another matter. He and his father did not agree about school. On many days, Pablo refused to attend. Don José had to take a firm grip on Pablo's hand and walk him to the school door. When Pablo finally did take a seat in class, he would draw or simply daydream. He did his best to ignore the teacher.

Something had to be done. After a few months of public school, Don José enrolled Pablo in Colegio San Rafaelo, a private school run by a family friend. Pablo agreed to attend, on the condition that he could take one of his father's pigeons with him. In class, the teacher allowed Pablo to sit behind the raised lid of his desk, hidden from other students, and spend his day drawing the pet bird.

5

When he grew tired of drawing, he would wander to a window and tap on the pane to attract the attention of people in the street. Sometimes he left the classroom and took refuge in the principal's nearby living quarters. There, the principal's pleasant wife allowed the boy to follow her about as she did her chores.

Pablo said later that he never drew stick figures, lollipop trees, or other "childish" art. Under the influence of his father's realistic style, Pablo tried from the beginning to draw exactly what he saw.

To the delight of Lola, his cousins, and friends, Pablo could put his pencil anywhere on a sheet of paper and draw whatever was requested with one line. He never hesitated. He never lifted his pencil.

It seemed like magic to his audience. Pablo could also take a pair of scissors and, with no lines to guide him, cut out horses, bulls, pigeons, or anything else his friends might request.

Although his work with pen and pencil was realistic from the start, whenever he used colors, he became as bold and innocent as any other child. This trait was to appear again and again in his work.

Pablo's parents knew at once that their son was a prodigy. Fortunately, Don José was able to provide everything—brushes, paints, canvas, sound advice, and encouragement.

At the age of eight, Pablo did *Toreador on Horseback,* his first oil painting. With remarkable confidence and skill, he depicted the horseman in the bullring, circling before the cheering crowd. Although awkward and unpolished compared with his work a few years later, and although Lola punched eyeholes through the canvas with a nail, Pablo never parted with the painting.

In 1891, soon after a second sister, María de la Concepción, was born, the city of Málaga decided to eliminate Don José's job at the museum. This not only reduced his income

Pablo, at age seven, poses with his sister Lola, who was then three years old. The photo was taken in Málaga.

but also forced him out of the studio that had been provided him at the museum. Don José angrily applied for a transfer. He would later regret his decision, but the application was granted and he soon faced the prospect of moving to another city.

La Coruña, a port city on the windblown Atlantic coast, was about as far from Málaga as Don José could go without leaving Spain. The move meant trading a balmy Mediterranean climate for the fog, rain, and wind of the north. Worst of all, it meant saying farewell to countless relatives and lifelong friends. But in September, he and Doña María, with their three children, boarded a boat for the far side of Spain. The baby was just six months old. Lola was six years old. Pablo was almost ten.

Don José began work as a professor of ornamental and figure drawing at La Coruña's provincial art school, Instituto da Guarda. Luckily, he was able to find an apartment across the street from the school, but Don José was unhappy from the start. Without friends to find commissions for him, there was little hope of selling even an occasional painting. The school and the city were both strange. The people, wary of outsiders, did little to welcome the new art teacher and his family. He felt like an alien.

Don José enrolled Pablo in elementary school classes at the institute. Here the father could keep an eye on him. But Pablo stubbornly refused to learn a thing in class. He just drew. In every spare moment, he drew. His teachers let the stubborn boy have his way. This continued for a year. As an adult, Pablo would confess that he was never sure of the order of the alphabet; even simple arithmetic was a mystery.

The unusual treatment in school set Pablo apart from the other pupils. He missed developing normal relationships. Although, in later years, he was able to overcome his lack of formal instruction, he often showed immature traits in his relationships with other people. He had many friends, but even those closest to him often found him difficult and unpredictable.

Fortunately, an elementary school education at the time was not required in Spain. Don José, however, insisted that Pablo pass the elementary-school test. As Pablo remem-

8

bered, it was a sham. He simply copied a column of numbers from the blackboard, something he could do easily, and when his examiner conveniently left the room, he copied the answer from the teacher's desk. Thus, he turned in a column of figures with the correct total. It was enough to satisfy his father. In October 1892, Don José enrolled Pablo in drawing classes. The boy's formal art instruction at last began.

The school followed age-old traditions for teaching art. Students began by drawing plaster casts of classical statues. Weeks might be spent drawing a plaster hand or arm. The method provided sound technical training, but it did nothing to encourage the imagination.

Although the drawings and paintings Pablo did outside class, depicting real bullfights, real birds and animals, and real people, were far more exciting and lively than the drawings of plaster casts, Pablo's teachers repeatedly cited him for excellence. At this time, he began keeping a diary combined with a daybook of sketches. By the end of the family's four-year stay in La Coruña, he had filled seventeen sketchbooks with drawings. He would continue filling sketchbooks for the rest of his career.

Pablo missed his friends and family in Málaga, but he did not like to write letters. Soon, however, he thought of a way to keep in touch. He made a Sunday newspaper—a folded sheet carrying short "articles" and drawings that dealt with La Coruña's current events. Usually, the major event was bad weather. One drawing showed heavily bundled women dipping their feet in the surf. It was captioned HOW PEOPLE BATHE . . . A weather report said: *The rain has begun. It will go on till summer.* Another said: *The wind is blowing and will go on blowing till La Coruña blows away.*

Although Pablo hated the climate, he liked his teachers. Their old-fashioned methods and the exacting demands could stifle average students, but Pablo accepted each class assignment as a challenge. By March of 1895, he finally

9

entered the studio where students were allowed to draw from nature—real people, real things, exactly what he had been doing at home ever since he could hold a pencil.

His production was remarkable. He worked with pencil, pen, watercolors, and oils. His brush strokes were swift and sure. His father saw his own modest talents being eclipsed by his son's genius and energy. It was during the La Coruña period, according to a story Pablo later told, that Don José handed his son all his brushes and his paints and vowed never to paint again.

Actually, Don José probably did not forsake painting entirely, but during his stay in La Coruña, he rarely painted at home. He was more moody and introspective than ever. He spent much of his spare time at a window, staring at the endless rain. He seemed to have no enthusiasm.

On January 5, 1895, tragedy struck. María de la Concepción, "Conchita," age four, died of diphtheria. The family was devastated. Don José felt he could no longer stay in this strange, unfriendly town that had brought nothing but sorrow. He applied for another transfer and soon was offered a job teaching in the School of Fine Arts in Barcelona, a major city on the northeast coast of Spain.

It was a change, and any change would be an improvement. He had to take the post at once. So, in March of 1895, leaving his family temporarily in La Coruña, he went to Barcelona to complete the school term. When summer came, he returned to take them to Málaga for a welcomed rest. It was a summer of happy reunion.

Pablo showed his sketchbooks everywhere. Uncle Salvador loved the drawings and was convinced that Pablo would be famous. He gave the boy an allowance and provided studio space in a room of the health inspection bureau. He even provided an old sailor to sit as a model. Pablo produced a portrait at once and was soon looking for other subjects.

Pablo's best work of the summer was a portrait of his eccentric Aunt Pepa. The old woman lived alone in an apartment cluttered with religious symbols and souvenirs. She rarely allowed visitors, and she rebuffed early requests to pose for Pablo. But one day she abruptly changed her mind and appeared, wearing a fur coat and all her jewelry.

Pablo reluctantly left the plaza where he was playing with Lola to do the portrait. It took him less than an hour, but he captured the character of the devout old woman perfectly.

Pablo did several portraits of his father. They were not flattering. Don José appears as a tired man with little hope or ambition.

There was, however, still hope and ambition for his son. Before the vacation ended, Don José took Pablo on a special trip to Madrid, the capital of Spain, to show his talented son works by Spain's most renowned artists—Zurbarán, Velázquez, El Greco, Goya, and many others.

In the great Prado, Pablo saw Velázquez's puzzling *Las Meninas (Maids of Honor)*, a large masterpiece in which Spain's royal family poses in the dark interior of a palace. It would one day inspire Pablo to do a remarkable series of paintings.

Don José declared that the works in the Prado represented Pablo's classical heritage, a heritage he must always respect and never abandon. Pablo was impressed, but he was also fourteen, a rebellious age. He was ready to question tradition. Despite what his teachers and his father believed, tradition might not hold all the answers.

Late in September 1895, the family left Málaga by boat for a leisurely cruise up the Mediterranean coast to Barcelona, the capital of Spain's Catalonia district. In this cosmopolitan city, artists had been challenging tradition for several years. The mood was restless. Change was in the air. Pablo could not have arrived in Barcelona at a better time.

2

---✘---

BARCELONA

Barcelona sputtered with political unrest. Republicans protested against a royal government. Separatists protested against a central government. Anarchists protested against any government. There were demonstrations and riots, fights and endless arguments.

The spirit of protest influenced Barcelona's writers, musicians, and artists. There was also a strong foreign influence. The artists in Barcelona, more than those in other Spanish cities, knew what was happening in studios, galleries, and museums elsewhere in Europe.

Conservatives viewed Barcelona as an embarrassment. While the rest of Spain remained faithful to the traditions of color, perspective, shading, and reality that had ruled for more than five centuries, Barcelona sought change. One daring painter had created a scandal by using blue in his shadows. It was something a Frenchman might do, but it was unheard of in Spain.

But what was worse, Barcelona artists dared to paint portraits that did not flatter their subjects. Cruel reality was considered bad taste. Other rebels painted unimportant people and events, even street scenes, showing ordinary peasants and shopkeepers. One artist devoted a whole canvas to a dead fish.

The Barcelona artists explained that they wanted their work to appeal more to the emotions than to the intellect. When they painted a portrait, they wanted to show more than their subject's appearance. They wanted the person's character or mood to come across to the viewer. If this meant painting faces that seemed unreal, then so be it.

Modern artists in Barcelona and elsewhere in Europe liked to point out that the camera was changing the role of the artist. If reality was all you wanted, they said, then take a photo of your subject and be done with it.

Although Don José believed in experimentation, he was shocked by Barcelona's modern ideas. Pablo was entranced.

Actually, the Barcelona moderns were not nearly as revolutionary as the young painters in Paris. There, the modern movement had been under way for twenty or thirty years. It began when a few painters produced "flat" pictures that had no shadows to suggest rounded forms, no perspective, no sense of depth. These painters defended their work by saying that they were using a flat canvas and to make the surface look like something else was not being honest. A flat picture was more real than a realist one.

This argument, of course, outraged the traditionalists.

Before that were the impressionists, a group of French artists who tried to capture the exact way the human eye saw color and light. Although conservative artists resisted this innovation, impressionist paintings gradually gained attention. They had wider and wider influence on young artists everywhere.

Although Barcelona's vigorous art colony was the most modern and bohemian in all of Spain, the city's School of Fine Arts still held staunchly to tradition.

Don José moved his family into an apartment at 4 Calle de Llauder. It was not far from the docks, and it was within walking distance of the school. Pablo immediately applied for entrance.

Although he was later to boast that he completed the entrance examination in one day, the fact was that Pablo took it in three separate sessions. The first day, he had to copy a picture. The second day, he had to draw a plaster cast. And the third day, he had to draw from a live model. He passed all three tests easily and, at age fourteen, became the youngest student in his class.

The Barcelona School of Fine Arts, known informally as La Lonja, or Stock Market, because it was housed in the stock market building, followed the same classical methods that Pablo had encountered at Málaga and La Coruña. Although he did not at first rebel against his assignments, he did complete them in a hurry so that he could spend most of his time on his own imaginative creations. He painted street scenes, landscapes, and portraits. He loved to wander down to the busy docks and watch the sailors and stevedores at work. He also roamed into other regions of the city, eager to learn all he could about his new home. He quickly learned Catalan, the dialect of the region.

La Lonja's faculty was headed by Antonio Cuba, one of Barcelona's top portrait artists. He recognized Pablo's talent at once and encouraged him to try some self-portraits. *Self-Portrait with Wig*, now in Barcelona's Picasso Museum, was painted during his first year at La Lonja.

His fellow students were more stimulating than any Pablo had known before. Although Manuel Pallarés y Grau was five years older, he and Pablo had much in common. Pallarés, who grew up in the small mountain village of Horta, was also a newcomer to Barcelona. Both found the city exciting and wonderful. The two became best friends. Pablo frequently brought Pallarés home, where he was treated as a member of the family.

Being among older students helped Pablo mature quickly. He had almost reached his full height now—five feet, three inches, but his short stature did not seem to bother him. Years later, Pallarés would recall that Pablo had not acted or looked like a boy in his early teens. His talent, of course, gave him confidence, but to be accepted by older students he had to act older than his years.

While Pablo took quickly to new surroundings and new friends, his father remained an outsider. Although the Barcelona climate was far better than La Coruña's, its people far friendlier, and its art community far more stimulating, Don José's mood did not brighten.

He feared that Pablo would get too much stimulation from the wrong sources. The young man was compulsive and unpredictable. To Don José, it would be a tragedy if Pablo wasted his remarkable talent in some outrageous modern movement. The father had already tried to tell Pablo that one did not have to wear funny clothes to be a painter.

It soon seemed that Don José's fears were justified. Pablo was growing restless with school assignments. He asked for more freedom, but Professor Cuba, with Don José's approval, decided that Pablo could profit from more discipline. One drawing Pablo did during this period was marked with an *E,* for excellent, six times and an *F,* for failure, four times. Don José himself had graded the work.

Pablo looked elsewhere for new challenges. He decided to

do something that was unheard of for a fifteen-year-old art student. He would start submitting paintings in some of Barcelona's group-show competitions.

Surprisingly, Don José agreed with the plan. He may have guessed that Pablo would go ahead, with or without his approval. Also, he probably wanted some control over what Pablo submitted.

Pablo prepared for the competitions in a very traditional frame of mind. He knew that they were firmly controlled by the old guard. He and his father chose subjects that were sure to appeal to the sentiments of traditional judges, and Pablo used a subdued pallet with only a few hints of impressionist colors. He painted three canvases.

Don José's favorite, *Science and Charity*, showed a sick woman being attended at her bedside by a doctor and a nun.

Two others, *First Communion* and *The Choirboy*, showing innocent youths in acts of devotion, were even more sentimental. In April 1896, the judges for Barcelona's Third Municipal Exposition of Fine Arts selected *First Communion* to hang in room one of the municipal gallery. It was an impressive achievement for the young artist. Don José glowed with pride. Pablo, who had priced the work at fifteen hundred pesetas, hoped that it would sell. It did not, but an art critic commented that young Ruiz-Picasso's work showed "sensitivity in the characters and firmness in the sketching of certain parts."

Science and Charity was to win even more attention. Pablo and Don José entered it in the 1897 Madrid General Fine Arts Exhibition. It was accepted and won an honorable mention. Later, it received the gold medal in the Provincial Exhibition at Málaga. There, his aunts, uncles, and cousins could see firsthand how his work had progressed.

In Barcelona, meanwhile, after the close of the first school year, Don José moved his family to the second floor of a building at 3 Calle de la Merced. He and Pablo could still

16

easily walk to school, and, halfway between school and their new home, Don José found space for a studio. Don José rented it and handed the keys to Pablo. It was a grand gesture and a proud event for both father and son. Without a doubt, Pablo had arrived.

When the fall term began, he was among the first to take part in pranks and parties. School friends recalled that he might be laughing one moment and moody and sad the next. He could lose his temper in a flash, but his anger would pass just as quickly as it came. The unpredictable mood changes, however, had long been part of his character. Now, with maturing confidence, he began to indulge other traits.

He loved costumes and masks, and he particularly enjoyed Barcelona's pre-Lenten festival with its street parades and revels. Self-portraits in costume or disguise began to appear along with the landscapes, street scenes, and religious pictures. He usually tried to make himself appear older than his fifteen years.

In later life, Pablo liked to brag that he became a painter with little formal art training, but this simply was not true. His father's early guidance, his traditional exercises at La Coruña, and his teachers at La Lonja gave him a wealth of formal, highly disciplined training. Even though he would one day rebel against those traditional teaching methods, his own career, without the formal background, would have been handicapped.

Because he could do his assignments quickly, Pablo was able, all through school, to use the assignments as a springboard for more imaginative work of his own. No doubt, he taught himself a great deal through this extra work, but to claim that he was self-taught did not do justice to his father or his teachers.

When he began working in his own studio, however, he began to develop the independence that would one day become his strength.

17

Don José was a little fearful of Pablo's independent nature, but fears that his son would be illiterate had been put to rest. Pablo had become an avid reader. Thanks to his natural curiosity and his bohemian surroundings, he read everything, including modern poets and philosophers. He also kept up with current events by studying Barcelona's journals and newspapers. He could hold his own with fellow students in discussions of politics, religion, literature, music, or art.

Don José, however, was more than a little worried about the bohemian atmosphere, not to mention the liberal politics of Barcelona. Thus, he was delighted when Uncle Salvador, along with other Málaga relatives, offered to send Pablo to Madrid, where he could study at the famous San Fernando Academy, the best art school in Spain. Muñoz Degrain, the Málaga artist who had provided refuge at the time of the earthquake, was now teaching at the academy.

Pablo, who had already put down roots in Barcelona, was not sure he wanted to go to Madrid, but after a summer vacation in Málaga, where all his old friends and his relatives endorsed the plan, he agreed to give the academy a try.

He enrolled as a disciple of Don Muñoz. It was a disaster. Pablo, expecting new challenges for his talent and energy, was shocked to be faced with the same old exercises that had dominated his first days at art school. He did not want to spend weeks on end drawing plaster casts. Don Muñoz, who had expected an innocent youth, eager for advice and guidance, was puzzled and even angered by Pablo's confidence and skill. Moreover, the boy had too much imagination, too much independence to fit into San Fernando's age-tested traditions.

Needless to say, Pablo and Don Muñoz did not become friends.

For several weeks, Pablo attended classes regularly, but he

found he profited more from the time he spent at the Prado, Spain's national museum, which had been introduced to him by his father. There, Pablo could stand before works of El Greco, Zurbarán, Velázquez, Goya, Titian, Van Dyck, Rubens, and scores of others.

Madrid was cold and wet. Pablo missed his friends, but he stayed in school to please his family. His patience, however, was wearing away.

The break came during a class field trip to Toledo, where each student was asked to copy El Greco's famous *Burial of Count Orgaz.* It is a large church painting, crowded with many figures. Below, the count's earthly friends are shown lowering his body into the grave. In the upper half of the picture, angels and other spirits are shown receiving the count's soul into the arch of heaven.

Pablo's copy was faithful in every detail except that he replaced some of El Greco's faces with portraits of several academy teachers and pupils. His teacher saw nothing at all funny in Pablo's adaptation, nor did he appreciate the young man's obvious skill. Instead, he went into a rage that drove Pablo from the classroom. He never returned.

The Prado now became his classroom. There, he could spend day after day copying paintings by Velázquez and El Greco. If weather permitted, he preferred to draw or paint from life outside. He filled five sketchbooks with Madrid street scenes, musicians, women arguing, peddlers, and buildings. He experimented with many styles, going from harsh realism to abstract shapes resembling arabesque patterns of Oriental rugs.

Lack of money became a problem. As long as Pablo was at the academy, Uncle Salvador provided a generous allowance, but when Pablo dropped out, the money stopped coming. Don José helped as best he could, but Pablo was forced to skip some meals and live in unheated attics. In the spring, he came down with scarlet fever. Pride kept him from telling his family. They knew nothing of his illness until June, when he appeared in Barcelona, pale and gaunt.

Pablo declared that he would never return to the academy. Uncle Salvador and other relatives in Málaga answered that the boy could expect no further help from them. Don José did not know what to do. Pablo wanted to be allowed to work on his own in his own studio. Don José did not think the boy could support himself. He needed more training. Pablo shook his head.

They did agree on one thing. Nothing could be done or decided until Pablo recovered his health.

His friend Pallarés, about to return for the summer to his mountain home at Horta, made a suggestion. Why didn't Pablo come with him? Mountain air and country cooking were certain to restore his strength, and he would have plenty of time to think about the future.

It turned out to be the perfect solution and an ideal holiday. The stay at Horta became a pivotal point in Pablo's career.

3

—⋈—

THE DROPOUT

In Catalan, *horta* means "garden." Although the land was rugged and often steep, crops flourished wherever the farmers could turn the soil and provide water. Uncultivated soil, baked hard in the sun, and the peaks of bare rock, which rose above the valley, made a stark contrast with the vines and olive trees and the terraced patches of garden.

Pablo had never known rural Spain. He had had no idea how hard people had to struggle to make a living on the land. At Horta, he developed a sincere respect for the Spanish peasant.

The village was more than a hundred miles southwest of Barcelona. Although Pablo and Manuel traveled at first by train, they had to complete their journey on a mountain trail, with mules carrying their luggage.

The Pallarés family gave the two young men an enthusiastic welcome. Manuel had two brothers, José and Salvador, and a sister, Carmen. Although Pablo was still a little weak when he arrived, his health returned quickly and he was soon enjoying family picnics and long hikes.

Horta was a new world. The farmers and herdsmen and their families, though struggling for survival, were friendly and honest. The peasants had skills that were strange and fascinating. Pablo learned how to saddle a pack mule and yoke oxen. He asked endless questions about making wine and olive oil, about planting and irrigation, about managing sheep and cattle. Years later, Pablo would often say that everything he knew he had learned at Horta.

He did not neglect his own skills. Pablo filled the pages of his sketchbook with drawings of peasants. He depicted them working, resting in the shade, or sitting in the cool haven of a local café. He also drew goats, cattle, horses, and donkeys. His lines are fluid and confident. Later, he painted some portraits of peasants.

To escape the heat, Pablo and Manuel camped in the mountains, where they drew or painted landscapes. Salvador, the youngest of the brothers, sometimes came with them, leading a pack mule with enough provisions to stay out several days. In the intense heat of summer, they took refuge in mountain caves.

They cooked their simple meals over an open fire. If necessary, Salvador was always willing to lead the mule down to the village for more food. They stored their supplies in an abandoned farmhouse that also provided shelter from the rain.

It was a great, romantic adventure. After city life, Pablo appreciated the freedom of the country.

In many talks with peasants, Pablo perfected his Catalan dialect. He could soon speak it like a native. This was important. He wanted to be accepted by these people.

Pablo and Manuel discussed art at length. They also talked

about the future. Pablo knew he had much to learn. But school, he decided, had nothing more to offer. He had been to Madrid and had attended the best school in Spain. It was stifling.

From now on, Pablo declared, he would have to teach himself. He would study the work of the masters. He would talk to other artists and observe their techniques. And he would paint, paint, and paint. He was sure he could learn more from experience than he could from the classroom.

Pallarés agreed that Pablo had already advanced far beyond anything an art school could offer. But Pablo knew that Don José would oppose the first suggestion of independent study.

Pablo delayed the confrontation with Don José as long as he could. He extended his vacation at Horta until February 1899.

When he finally faced his family with his decision, Don José reacted just as expected. He insisted that Pablo enroll for another term at La Lonja. Pablo refused. Don José was stunned. The boy had changed. He had, after all, been away for a long time. Except for a brief stay in June, Pablo had been free of Don José's influence for eighteen months. Change had to be expected.

Pablo was more serious, more intense, more confident than before, and he was fully committed to a career as an artist.

Don José appealed to Pallarés. Could he help change Pablo's mind? Manuel shook his head. Pablo wanted to begin making his own way. It would be best to let him find out if he could. Don José refused to turn his son loose in the city, and Pablo did agree to live at home at least for a few months.

Political unrest in Barcelona had increased. Poverty drove many into the streets to beg. War veterans swelled unemployment. There was talk of revolt. Anarchy was becoming almost respectable. All this worried Don José, but Pablo, although his sympathies were with the poor, did not become involved in politics. He was too dedicated to art to let anything distract him.

Although he avoided a complete break with his family, the atmosphere at home could be tense and uncomfortable, particularly in the evenings when his father was home. Pablo began spending his evenings at a new café that had opened near the Plaza Catalonia during his absence.

It was called the Four Cats, after a local proverb: "There will only be us four cats," which was another way of saying "We can't draw a crowd." The place, however, was almost always jammed with Barcelona's young intellectuals. A spirit of fun and informality dominated the atmosphere. There was a stage for puppet shows and shadow plays. Poets read their latest works. Musicians played recent compositions. Young artists hung their most outrageous drawings and paintings on the walls.

The café was the inspiration of Père Romeu, who had lived in Paris and Chicago. He wanted an establishment with an international atmosphere that would attract Barcelona's young journalists, poets, playwrights, musicians, sculptors, and painters.

Don José, of course, did not approve of the Four Cats. The place crawled with bohemians and anarchists. But, for Pablo, it was a haven where he could meet people who shared his hopes and ideas. Because of his talent, he won the respect and the friendship of many artists a good deal older than he. Many of Pablo's lifelong friendships began at the Four Cats.

Josep Cardona, a young sculptor, had a brother who owned an apartment. There was a spare room on the mezzanine. Would Pablo like to have it for a studio? Pablo accepted the offer at once. The rest of the building was occupied by workers who made corsets and other undergarments. As a diversion from art, Pablo liked to operate the machine that made eyelets in corsets.

Although Pablo's room was tiny, he soon began receiving

24

visitors. Other artists wanted to see what the promising young man was doing. Poets and writers also came to see Pablo's recent sketches and paintings.

Carlos Casagemas stopped often at the studio, and he and Pablo frequently appeared at the Four Cats together. An up-and-coming painter, Casagemas was Pablo's physical opposite. He was as tall and thin as Pablo was short and stocky. Carlos wore high, stiff collars and side whiskers, which called attention to his receding chin and remarkably long, pointed nose. Despite their physical differences, the two found that they had a great deal in common.

A year older than Pablo, Casagemas had been slated for a career in the navy, but Spain's defeat in the Spanish-American War changed that plan. Actually, he had more enthusiasm for painting than he did for a military life, but he did remain fascinated with firearms and other military weapons.

Jaime Sabartés, a long-haired poet, on his first visit to Pablo's studio, was amazed both by the quality of the paintings and drawings and by the young painter's powerful personality. Years later, Sabartés recalled that he had to resist bowing in respect before Pablo when they said good-bye at the end of that first meeting. Throughout their long friendship, Sabartés would continue to worship Pablo.

Pablo also visited other artists in their studios, and he became a regular visitor on Sunday afternoons at the Pallarés apartment, where he and other friends argued, sang, recited poetry, and drank coffee laced with flaming rum.

All the social activities, however, were secondary to work. Pablo was tireless. Although he was enjoying life fully in this first period of real independence, his work was often filled with sadness. One major painting depicts a procession of old people shuffling down the road to death. He also painted a sorrowing couple in a dark room, saying good-bye. Perhaps Barcelona's poverty influenced this work, but he was more influenced by Northern Europeans, who were dealing at the time with macabre subjects.

In addition to the sad pictures, however, he also painted spirited portraits and faces inspired by classical Greek sculpture. His *Young Girl in White Near a Window* shows his sister, Lola, silhouetted against the golden glow of sunlight. It is as happy as the other pictures are sad.

Working in two or more contrasting styles or moods almost simultaneously became a standard pattern for Picasso. He also liked to vary his materials. Although he was then painting mostly in oils, he perfected his use of pastels as well. It was as if one style or medium, by contrast, stimulated another entirely different style or medium.

In Barcelona, the only modern gallery was Sala Parés, which was just beginning to show impressionist paintings. In Paris, impressionism had become old-fashioned. Pablo and his more serious friends were aware of their own limitations. One day, they agreed, they would have to visit Paris, perhaps even live there.

At the moment, however, the luxury of travel seemed a long way off. Barely on speaking terms with his father, Pablo had moved out of the apartment. Although he never had a total break with his family, further financial help could hardly be expected.

He slept in his studio or with a friend. He had also discovered Barcelona's many brothels. It was not unusual, when business was slow, for Pablo to spend the night with one of the prostitutes. A painting or a drawing was usually all the pay necessary. In one brothel where he stayed for several weeks, he covered the walls of one room with murals.

The portraits he did of the prostitutes were rarely flattering. Usually he depicted them with a cruel reality that left no hint of tenderness or sympathy.

The women, however, influenced him greatly. A new girl often triggered a new burst of creative energy. His sexual appetite seemed to be just as urgent as his need to paint. Sometimes the effect of a new woman would produce an entirely new style of painting, a style that would dissipate in time, as the romance cooled. This link between sexual exploits and creativity was another pattern that developed in these early days. It would continue throughout most of Pablo's life.

Although he was surrounded by many companions at this time, Pablo's closest friend was Carlos Casagemas. Early in 1900, they began sharing a studio. It was a large, unfurnished room with wide windows on the top floor of an old house at 17 Calle Riera. They decorated the walls with pictures of chairs, a table, and a sofa. On one wall they painted shelves, a counter, and all the clutter of a pantry. On another, they painted an open closet. They even painted a safe on one wall.

Actually, Casagemas received a generous allowance from his parents. He paid the rent and was always willing to cover other expenses. He also was an avid listener when Pablo spoke of his hopes and ideas. This trait alone endeared him to Pablo.

On Sunday afternoons, Casagemas's parents opened their home to provide a favorite gathering spot for all their son's bohemian friends. For entertainment, the youths would act out ideas on the spur of the moment in a sort of Spanish charades. The most popular pastime for the artists in the crowd, however, was "fried drawings," produced by dipping their drawings in a pan of sizzling oil to get bizarre distortions and textures.

In February 1900, Pablo finally agreed to show his work at the Four Cats. His drawings were mostly portraits of friends and café clientele. There was just one painting. It showed a priest at the bedside of a dying woman. The show was reviewed in a daily paper by a writer who said that the drawings had character and the painting had qualities that

27

were not to be sneered at. It was an unusually long review for a young, unknown artist, but the reviewer misspelled Pablo's name, referring to him as "Mr. Ruiz Picazzo." Just the same, Pablo's friends were delighted. The drawings, priced at a few pesetas, sold briskly, mostly to the people Pablo had depicted.

Soon after this modest success, Pablo tried to earn some money by giving drawing lessons, but he attracted just one student and abandoned the effort.

Good news, however, soon came from Paris. He had entered several works to be considered for inclusion in the Spanish section of the Universal Exposition to be held in Paris in the fall. One of his oils, *Last Moments,* had been accepted.

This not only gave Pablo his first recognition outside of Spain, but it also provided him with a good reason to go to Paris. The show, which would include a hundred-year survey of contemporary painting, was to be held in the Grand Palais. It would be an important show, and Pablo was determined to see it. He also wanted to go to all the museums and galleries he had been reading about.

He began making plans. Casagemas decided to go to Paris with him. Pallarés, who could not leave at once, would join them in the city later. Another artist offered the three young men his Paris studio.

Meanwhile, in a burst of energy, Pablo began painting pictures of bullfights, city streets, and other Spanish scenes he believed would appeal to Paris galleries. He wanted his work to be seen in what was then the art capital of the world.

The acceptance of Pablo's oil in the Paris show caused some envy among several Barcelona artists, particularly the older, established painters who had been unable to get in. There was a good deal of protest over the selection of an eighteen-year-old boy's work. The protests, however, only called attention to Pablo's talent. Two Barcelona magazines that had previously rejected his work now printed his drawings. It seemed that he was finding recognition at last, but a long struggle still lay ahead.

4

THE BLUE PERIOD

Although his first trip to Paris in the fall of 1900 was brief, it was an important step in Pablo's development. He was not quite nineteen years old when he arrived in Montmartre, the bohemian section of the city that once had been a hillside covered with windmills, vineyards, and rock quarries.

The city was expanding. The land had become too valuable for vineyards. Wheat was now milled by steam engines. Many of the windmills, or *moulins,* had been converted into cafés and nightclubs. Casagemas and Pablo moved into a friend's studio at 49, rue Gabrielle and immediately began looking up acquaintances. Many Spanish expatriots were living in Montmartre. They served as interpreters for the two young painters.

At the exhibition, Pablo stood before original works of

Manet, Cézanne, Toulouse-Lautrec, and many other moderns. He studied them with admiration. He also roamed the galleries of the Louvre and other museums. For the first time, he saw the works of Jean Ingres and Eugène Delacroix. Ingres was a neoclassical painter. Delacroix was a romantic. Pablo admired them both. He also was moved by the postimpressionists Paul Gauguin, Vincent van Gogh, Henri de Toulouse-Lautrec, and Edgar Degas. He studied scores of original works by these men.

Pablo could take in a picture quickly, and his memory was remarkably accurate. When he saw one he admired, it became a permanent fixture in his mind. The Paris museums polished Pablo's education.

Pablo also met many artists and art dealers. A few days after his arrival, he visited Berthe Weill's small gallery. There, he had the good luck to meet Pedro Manach, a Spanish industrialist, who had begun dealing in art. He offered Pablo one hundred fifty francs (about thirty dollars) a month for all the work he could produce. Pablo promptly accepted the offer.

Meanwhile, Berthe Weill paid Pablo one hundred francs for three of his bullfight pictures. She resold them at once at a profit of fifty francs.

Although both transactions were small, they boosted Pablo's confidence and suggested that it would be wise to visit Paris again and perhaps stay longer.

Although his contacts were limited by his lack of French, he soon began picking up practical words from the prostitutes who could always be found in the Montmartre cafés. After Pallarés arrived, he, Casagemas, and Pablo went to the circus and visited all the cafés and dance halls of Montmartre. There, Pablo got the inspiration for his first Paris paintings.

Le Moulin de la Galette, *Can Can*, and *Stiff Shirts* were inspired by Toulouse-Lautrec, both in subject matter and

31

style. Pablo said later that he had had to go to Paris to realize how great Lautrec's talent had been. Pablo, however, did not picture Montmartre's night spots as the joyful places Lautrec had portrayed. Pablo's works had a somber, even tragic, view. Although he had little respect for the entertainers and the prostitutes, he did think they were being exploited.

Casagemas, meanwhile, fell in love with Germaine, one of the café girls who had posed for the three artists. Germaine did not return the affection and drove Casagemas to distraction. Pablo did not understand how anyone could get so upset over a girl. But Casagemas, as events would prove, was tragically smitten.

Thanks to Manach's support, the three young artists had enough spending money to enjoy the nightlife. Manach himself benefited. During or soon after Pablo's first stay in Paris, Manach sold seven paintings, including *Le Moulin de la Galette*, for a grand total of 695 francs (about $140).

Pablo, who had been signing his pictures "P. Ruiz Picasso," now began using "P. R. Picasso." Ruiz, his father's name, was common, but Picasso, his mother's maiden name, was so unusual that it stuck in people's memories. Later, Pablo was to use "P. Picasso" and, finally, simply "Picasso."

In December, Pablo decided to return to Spain. There were several reasons. The lovesick Casagemas was talking about suicide. It would be best to get him away from Paris and Germaine. Picasso himself wanted to break off an affair with a Spanish prostitute, which had grown too serious. Furthermore, Paris had turned cold.

The studio was hard to heat. Barcelona would be far more comfortable. Better yet, why not visit Málaga? Perhaps, in Málaga, a city he had never seen, Casagemas might forget Germaine. Thus, the two artists stayed only briefly in Barcelona before continuing south to Pablo's native city and his relatives.

The relatives did not know how to receive the two untidy,

long-haired young men. Pablo's favorite costume at this time was a floppy hat, a long coat of great age, and a walking stick. It raised no eyebrows in Barcelona or Paris, but in Málaga it left people gaping. The city had never before been exposed to bohemian artists. Uncle Salvador did not try to hide his displeasure, and several others in his family were cool to Pablo and his friend. Pablo was amused, but he loved his relatives deeply and remained calm and attentive. He saw them all. Casagemas was uncomfortable, and, saying he could no longer live without Germaine, he soon left for Paris.

Pablo stayed on, visiting bars and brothels, sketching, and shocking friends and the relatives. He could not decide what to do. For a time he talked of going to London, but finally he decided on Madrid.

Money was again a problem. He had received no money from Manach for several weeks, for the simple reason that he had sent Manach no pictures. In Madrid, Pablo found a loft with space enough to work. Fried eggs, he said later, were all he could afford to eat, but his major concern was the winter cold. With no money for coal, the loft was too cold for sleep. He took refuge in cafés and brothels.

In later years, Pablo claimed that he had lived by begging. Undoubtedly, he took advantage of generous prostitutes and café owners, but he also had enough money for paints, eggs, and other necessities. At one point he took a trip to Toledo to see the El Grecos again.

In Madrid, a writer he had known in Barcelona decided to start a magazine. *Arte Joven (Young Art)* would introduce Madrid to modern ideas. The first of five issues appeared on March 10, 1901. It and the ones that followed were amply illustrated with drawings taken mostly from Pablo's Paris sketchbooks.

The magazine, which endorsed radical politics and philosophies, had no trouble getting contributions of poetry and articles from Madrid's young writers, but it had much trouble getting subscribers and advertisers. The final issue appeared in June. By then, Pablo was no longer in Madrid. He had left the city in haste after hearing of the suicide of Casagemas.

Pablo did not learn the full details until he reached Barcelona and received a report from Pallarés, who had been with Casagemas in Paris.

The two of them, with several male and female friends, including Germaine, had gone to a café. Casagemas, unknown to anyone, had been carrying a pistol. Soon after the party had been seated, Casagemas had jumped up, gun in hand, and fired at Germaine. Pallarés had deflected his aim. The shot had missed, but Casagemas, thinking he had hit the girl, immediately pointed the gun at his head and fired. He died in a hospital a few hours later.

Pablo was stunned. He was already depressed by the poverty and discomfort of Madrid, and Casagemas's death moved him profoundly. Somehow, he found society in general at fault. At the same time, he wondered if there might have been something he could have done to prevent the tragedy. He still could not understand how a man could work himself into such a state over a woman.

Pablo's Barcelona friends, probably looking for a way to divert Pablo's mind from the death, organized a show for him at Sala Parés. Some friends later recalled that they hoped a successful show might persuade Pablo to settle in Barcelona. Pablo, however, was not enthusiastic. He selected some recent pastels and oils, mostly of women of the evening dressed in rich silks and jewels. The colorful costumes set off the animal sexuality of his models with cruel contrast. The works might cause controversy, but they certainly would not attract any buyers.

Meanwhile, word came from Paris of a far more exciting opportunity.

Ambroise Vollard, the art dealer for such pioneers of modernism as Cézanne and Gauguin, was interested in putting together a Picasso exhibit. Was Pablo interested?

Vollard's offer took Pablo's full attention and energy. He had no time for his Barcelona friends. He did little to prepare for the Sala Perés show, and when he learned that works of Ramon Casas, whom he had long seen as a rival, would be shown in the gallery at the same time, Pablo refused to attend the opening.

Despite Pablo's offhand attitude, the show brought praise from a critic. It was also the first time that the single name "Picasso" had appeared by itself and was correctly spelled in a critical review.

In June 1901, carrying a large collection of paintings and pastels and wearing a black beard and mustache, Pablo left Barcelona for his second stay in Paris. The agent Manach provided a spacious studio in a building at 130, boulevard de Clichy in Montmartre, in the same building where he lived. Several established artists lived nearby.

Ambroise Vollard, at the time, was the most eccentric art dealer in Paris. His small gallery on rue Laffitte was crowded with Gauguins, Renoirs, and Cézannes, works that less daring dealers would not touch. Vollard had been the first to show a collection of Cézanne's work. It caused a scandal. Critics saw the work as ugly daubs. The public did not buy. Today, just one small Cézanne cannot be had for less than $100,000.

Pablo was profoundly impressed by Vollard's Cézanne collection. He logged the works in his memory for future reference. Meanwhile, he spread out his own pastels and paintings for Vollard's inspection.

He had brought dozens of drawings and more than one hundred paintings. Vollard selected sixty-five works for a show, including bullfights, street scenes, nudes, nightlife paintings from Madrid, Barcelona, and Paris, and some portraits.

35

Vollard was attracted by Pablo's bold use of color, which filled his paintings with emotion.

There was a portrait of Manach painted with white, black, and yellow and an accent of red. It was done with vertical brush strokes that were too broad to allow much detail, but the painting was alive with emotion, and it was a good likeness of the dealer.

Although most critics ignored Pablo's show, several paintings were sold. Even those who did not buy viewed the young Spaniard's work with interest and approval. Vollard agreed to serve as Pablo's dealer and display his work regularly in the small gallery.

On July 15, 1901, the day after the show closed, there was a faint knock on Pablo's studio door. A shy poet had come to introduce himself. His name was Max Jacob. He thought Pablo's work was wonderful.

So far, Pablo's Paris friends had been Spaniards. Jacob was his first French friend. At the time, each knew only a few words of the other's language. Just the same, Jacob managed to convey his admiration and was invited into the large studio, which was crowded with Pablo's Spanish-speaking friends. It was an informal party. People sat on the floor, eating, drinking, and talking incessantly.

Before he left, Jacob invited everyone to his place the following night.

At Jacob's, Pablo and his friends appeared, to carry the drinking and talking far into the night. Pablo, however, remained long after the others had left. He painted Max's portrait, and Max gave Pablo a sixteenth-century woodcut. That first evening, Pablo and Max talked mostly in sign language.

Paris's many museums and art galleries delighted Pablo. On this visit, he was especially impressed by a show of Vincent van Gogh's work. It attracted little public attention, but Pablo and a few other young painters were fascinated.

Van Gogh's assertive brush strokes and passionate use of color encouraged Pablo to continue his own experiments with color.

At the same time, however, he began turning out somber canvases that were dominated by blue. The dark paintings were almost surely the result of sadness and remorse over Casagemas's suicide. It was during the summer of 1901 that he painted *The Burial of Casagemas,* a large oil with a split composition showing earthly figures below and heavenly figures, including the spirit of his friend, above. The composition was borrowed from El Greco's *Burial of Count Orgaz,* which also had been the basis for Pablo's schoolboy prank a few years before.

Although Pablo painted his figures in light earth tones, the blue in the background dominated. It was one of the first paintings to come from what would soon be known as Picasso's blue period. In the same summer, Pablo painted several death portraits of his friend, as well as pictures of the café where Casagemas had shot himself.

Neither Manach nor Vollard liked the direction Pablo was taking, but his pictures grew more somber. The blue shades darkened. The pessimistic works interested no one at the time, but for several months Pablo could paint no other way. It was as if his great sorrow could find release only on canvas. He did not care what anyone thought about those works.

He painted café scenes, concentrating on society's outcasts—the drunks, beggars, aging prostitutes, hungry families, and others down on their luck. The blue light that filled these paintings carried the full sadness of evening. The faces and limbs of his figures became elongated in Gothic distortion. Even when he painted portraits, he distorted features. Remarkably, he still made good likenesses of his subjects. The portraits, however, were not flattering. They were just as hard to sell as other blue-period pictures.

A self-portrait done at this time shows solid features, thick

One of Picasso's earliest etchings, **The Frugal Repast** *was made in 1904. It is a fine example of his blue period.* 18³/₁₆″ × 14¹³/₁₆″

black hair, a fringe of beard, hollow cheeks, and dark, sad eyes. It, too, was not flattering, but the emotional impact of the portrait says a great deal about Pablo's character. He was telling his friends that creativity was not possible without suffering. All his blue-period people seem to be suffering from unspeakable depression.

The mood of the period, however, was in conflict with Pablo's life-style. He was enjoying himself immensely. He loved the company of his friends. He delighted in his brief ventures with women. He was well fed, well entertained. And he had ample time and space for his work.

Jaime Sabartés, who had also come to Paris from Barcelona, had a room in the Latin Quarter, which became the evening headquarters for a widening circle of friends. Pallarés, Manach, Jacob, and the sculptors Mateo de Soto and Manolo became known as Pablo's Gang. They would sing, strum guitars, talk, and argue far into the night. At the end, all but Jacob, who was never comfortable with women, would cap off the evening by visiting a brothel.

The gang sometimes prowled through the toughest sections of Montmartre, looking for adventure. One street where a man was said to have been scalped by his enemies fascinated them. Here, they discovered a beer hall with dirt floors, empty barrels for furniture, and a proprietor who sang for his patrons. It became the gang's favorite hangout. They cleaned the place up, painted the walls white, and set Pablo to work with his oils. Soon the walls were decorated with blue nudes.

Max Jacob saw Pablo almost daily. The poet later said that he believed in Pablo more than in himself and an evening with the painter left him encouraged about life.

None of this, no hint of happiness or high spirits, however, showed in Pablo's work. Even after acrobats and other circus performers began to appear in his pictures, they seemed isolated in a sad world, cut off from hope or happiness. He also began painting pregnant women or women with children, often as part of larger family groups. These "maternities," as they were called, sustained the sadness of the blue period.

Today, in addition to Pablo's reaction to the Casagemas tragedy, we can see in the blue period the influence of other painters, including the geometric forms of Cézanne and the melancholy of Gauguin. Pablo had discovered these painters long before the public recognized their greatness. It is thus no surprise that the work of the blue period was also ahead of its time.

Several years later, long after Picasso had moved on to other styles, the blue-period paintings became highly prized. Unfortunately, the style was and still is imitated so frequently by lesser artists that it has become trite.

Inevitably, Pablo's relationship with Manach became strained. When the evening parties were held at Pablo's studio, as sometimes happened, the arguments, the singing, and the guitar strumming kept the art dealer awake far into the night. Manach, already upset with Pablo's current work, lost his enthusiasm for his fellow Spaniard.

The sloppy, unorganized state of the artist's studio made it difficult to locate anything. Manach frequently searched among the canvases that leaned haphazardly against walls and furniture. Always, everything was blue. He could find none of the colorful works that had been so successful at Vollard's.

Manach suggested that Pablo do more marketable work. Picasso refused. He did not like anyone to question his style or mood of the moment. Manach was at first puzzled. Later, he turned angry and withdrew his financial support for Pablo.

Meanwhile, Pablo's friendship with many members of the gang cooled. He grew aloof and began avoiding the evening parties. Toward the close of the year, he announced that he would soon return to Barcelona. All he was waiting for was a letter from his father with the train fare. The letter, when it finally came, may also have had important news about Pablo's draft status.

When he turned twenty in the fall of 1901, he became subject to three years of compulsory military service in Spain. Somehow he avoided it. Some said he drew a high number in the 1901 draft, but it is also possible that Uncle Salvador put up the money to excuse Pablo from service, a common practice at the time.

At any rate, in January 1902, Pablo returned to Barcelona to visit his family, without any fear of being taken into custody as a draft evader. It was not a triumphant return. He was broke, with nothing to show for six month of work but scores of paintings he could not sell.

5

THE ROSE PERIOD

Pablo was not sure he would ever return to Paris. The city had not defeated him, but his experience forced him to wonder if he belonged in France.

The blue paintings continued. If anything, the figures he painted became sadder, more listless than ever. He usually painted women, alone or with a child. They seemed to be using their last reserves of energy to stay alive. Timeless lassitude, mixed with a sense of loneliness and misery, make the Barcelona paintings the most memorable works of the blue period.

For the next several months, Pablo lived at home. He shaved off his beard, but he retained his drooping mustache. And he still dressed like a bohemian, trousers drawn in at the ankles, floppy hat, and colorful tie. Sabartés, who returned from Paris soon after Pablo, cut off his long hair.

Pablo and Sabartés still frequented dark cafés and brothels, but Pablo's life was growing more orderly. He rarely missed a day of work, usually painting for several hours at a time. And he tried to improve his relationship with his father.

When Don José said that Pablo was wasting his talent or that his current work would never make him famous or even make him a living, Pablo remained silent. This worried Doña Maria. Pablo usually defended himself loudly. Something had to be wrong.

Meanwhile, Pablo's interest in Paris revived. Berthe Weill had tried to sell the Picassos she had collected by giving a show in her gallery of the works of Spanish artists. The show was a failure. Manach had better luck selling Picasso drawings.

This news made Pablo restless. He did not want to be represented in Paris by work that was several months old. He wanted to be known for his current work.

In October of 1902, he persuaded Don José once again to give him train fare for Paris. Without Manach's support, Pablo had to rely on the charity of other artists to stay alive. He lived at first in a small loft in the Latin Quarter owned by a Spanish sculptor. The place had just one bed, forcing Pablo and the sculptor to take turns sleeping.

The loft was so small and cluttered that Max Jacob was shocked. On his first visit, the poet went out immediately for some potatoes in order to fry a meal for his friend. Max decided something had to be done. He had been eking out a living by part-time tutoring. He gave that up for a full-time job, and with his first paycheck, he rented a room large enough to share with Pablo.

Again there was only one bed, but Max worked all day and Pablo did not mind painting at night. Taking turns sleeping was thus not too inconvenient. They lived on eggs, potatoes, and beans, which they cooked on a burner in the small room.

They told themselves that this was all just temporary, but Pablo could not sell his paintings or drawings. Meanwhile, the demands of a full-time job were too much for Max. He did not think he could continue much longer.

Later, Max recalled, they both talked of suicide at this time. It easily could have been done by jumping out the window. Pablo, however, said suicide was never discussed.

But it is fairly certain that the two friends were facing starvation when the wife of a friend bought one of Pablo's pastels. Pablo abruptly said good-bye to Max, hurried to the train station, and bought a ticket for Barcelona.

Pablo would later talk nostalgically of his poverty at other times and other places, poverty that was actually more romantic than desperate, but he would not talk about the one time when he really faced starvation. It was too painful to recall. To his acute embarrassment, however, Max loved to tell their friends of those desperate days in Paris.

The experience had one good effect on Pablo. It gave him humility. He returned to Barcelona a more mature person.

Now sharing a studio with another artist in Barcelona, Pablo returned to his routine. Although twilight blues still dominated pictures of life-weary figures, the figures themselves were most usually portraits of people he saw on the streets or in cafés. Pablo could remember the features of a face so well that it was easy for him to draw or paint a likeness hours or even days later in his studio. His *Old Guitar Player*, which dates from this period, is undoubtedly based on a café musician Pablo knew. Occasionally, he gave up his blue palette to paint the Barcelona rooftops he saw from the studio window.

He joined Sabartés every evening. One night, with a brush dipped in blue paint, Pablo decorated the walls of Sabartés's apartment with murals. After Paris, Barcelona's nightlife seemed rather tame to both the poet and the painter, but when not painting, Pablo needed company. Often he and Sabartés passed the evenings alone.

Pablo had left several paintings and drawings with friends in Paris, in the hope that they could sell them, but the lack of news was depressing. Only Max Jacob wrote him, and to Pablo's amazement, Max's letters told about an affair he was having with a married woman. Max was too much in love to write about the Paris art market.

Early in 1904, a new theme began to appear in Pablo's pictures. Although his mood remained blue, he now depicted couples embracing. The figures were young. There were hints of vigor and hope. He also became interested in allegory, something the symbolist painters had explored at the close of the nineteenth century.

His large *La Vie (Life)* shows a man embraced by a naked woman, while a clothed woman, holding a child, stands close by, watching. The faces are without expression, but the meaning seems clear. The man is torn between physical love, symbolized by the naked woman, and ideal love, symbolized by the young mother. This ancient theme, the conflict between profane and sacred love, would appear repeatedly in Pablo's work for the next several years. It appealed to his love of paradox, and it incidentally reflected his own attitude toward women.

He once said that women were either doormats or goddesses. Sooner or later, he would treat most of the women in his life as doormats. Perhaps his limited schooling, which kept him from making friends early and delayed his social development, and his early association with prostitutes did not help to encourage a respect for women. Ironically, though, most women found him fascinating.

Some friends say that Casagemas's fatal involvement with Germaine contributed to Pablo's detached attitude. He could not make emotional commitments. His lovemaking was biological, nothing more than a physical release. When he did make long-term attachments, he seemed to be motivated more by convenience than love.

Pablo rarely showed his work at this time. He seemed to know it would not sell, at least not in Barcelona. He could easily have turned out fashionable paintings and made a comfortable living, but he was too proud to compromise. He had to paint for himself, and, as he told his friends, if he would not come to terms with public tastes, then public tastes would have to come to terms with him.

This, he realized, would never happen in Barcelona. He loved the city, but its citizens did not appreciate artistic independence. Paris was the only city where painters could develop their own style and survive. After his last experience, it took a great deal of courage for Pablo to return to Paris, but in April 1904, after reluctantly saying good-bye once again to his family and his friends, Pablo made the move. This time he was determined to give Paris a full test. He would stay at least a year. As it turned out, he stayed for forty-two years.

His first need was a cheap studio. His Paris friends directed him to Bateau-Lavoir or "Laundry Boat." It was a ramshackled, wooden building that hung to a Montmartre hillside. From the windows you could get a view of shacks, cheap tenements, cafés, beer gardens, and here and there a tree. Many of the residents took in laundry to earn money. The drying sheets flapping from the old structure did indeed make the building look like a ship under full sail.

Pablo took over a studio recently vacated by another Spaniard who left some easels, a mattress, a table, an old trunk, one chair, a washbowl, and an inefficient potbellied stove. Bateau-Lavoir occupants froze in the winter and boiled in the summer, but the rent was reasonable, often extremely reasonable. The manager did not live in the building. She never knew exactly who the tenants were. Artists moved in and out almost at will. Many never paid.

Max Jacob, who had survived his love affair, was among the first to welcome Pablo back. He at once offered to promote Pablo and began taking paintings and drawings to shops and galleries. Most people took one look and sent Max away. Vollard still refused to handle the blue canvases. Sometimes, however, the owner of a secondhand shop or an antique dealer would pay a few francs for a drawing. When Max sold something, he would convert the cash to bundles of groceries and return victoriously to Pablo's studio.

Pablo had discovered that it was easier to find friends among poets and writers than among other artists. He was in competition with other artists, but this was not the case with writers, and he liked the intellectual stimulation that the writers gave him. In neighboring cafés, he was introduced to Guillaume Apollinaire and André Salmon. Both men would become influential writers and close friends.

Pablo, still painting in blue, did most of his work at night. An oil lamp and perhaps a candle or two were all he needed to light his studio. When he went out, he donned a raincoat over his paint-stained blue overalls. He went to museums frequently. He felt more confident about his work, but he was sometimes lonely.

Soon after moving into Bateau-Lavoir, Pablo noticed a girl with a fine figure and a pretty face, who wore elegant dresses and hats whenever she left her nearby room. Pablo introduced himself at the first opportunity. The girl called herself Fernande Olivier. Years later, when describing their first meeting, she said she could hardly face the fire in Pablo's eyes.

They met often in the hallway, and one rainy day, after Pablo had rescued a kitten from the storm, he invited Fernande into his studio to dry the animal. Their affair began in the autumn of 1904. Fernande, however, did not move in with Pablo until early the following year.

Was Pablo at last in love? It is difficult to say, but we do know that his liaison with Fernande brought an abrupt change in his work.

The dark, somber blues lightened at last, giving way to pale browns, reds, and pinks. Although the people he depicted, mostly circus performers, still evoked sadness, they had more life than the outcasts of his blue paintings. These were not aging, listless people in attitudes of despair. His circus figures, melancholy and fragile as they might seem, were generally young and vibrant. There was less distortion, more classical proportion. Still, the figures retained enough unique features to make them seem like portraits of circus entertainers Pablo had seen.

The new style, now classified as Picasso's rose phase, was almost certainly inspired by his relationship with Fernande Olivier. In addition to changing his emotional outlook, her presence also changed his life-style. They lived like a conventional married couple, often staying home evenings, alone. The long evenings of drinking and smoking in Montmartre cafés and brothels were over.

Friends dropped by Pablo's studio less often, and when they did, they arrived and left sober. Fernande was a clever housekeeper. A few francs a day were all she needed to prepare meals. When Pablo got a little extra cash, he often bought a bottle of Fernande's favorite cologne rather than a bottle of wine.

Whenever possible, Max Jacob continued to sell Pablo's drawings and paintings to secondhand dealers and to convert the cash into groceries, but his studio visits were less frequent. He was still not comfortable around women, and Fernande was all woman.

Pablo spent more time at work. He painted several portraits of Fernande. The pictures reflect his bursting pride in

In Montmartre, Pablo and Fernande Olivier, his first mistress, lived the bohemian life in a small studio in Bateau-Lavoir. This photo was taken in 1906. RÉUNION DES MUSÉES NATIONAUX

having won a beautiful mistress. His pride was also obvious when they went out together. Pablo almost strutted.

His friends were amused. Fernande was statuesque, a good deal taller, and a few months older than Pablo. One friend said that Pablo looked like a student having an affair with his teacher. Pablo himself used to joke about Fernande's age, saying he was attracted to older women.

Work of the rose period promised to be more marketable, but he was not pandering to the public taste. He was still painting for himself. He turned down seven hundred francs at this time to do some illustrations for a popular humor magazine. He did make some posters to advertise plays, but they were not successful. He soon gave up the effort.

Works of the rose period are sometimes puzzling. While some of the first canvases, such as *The Actor* and *Seated Nude,* are straightforward studies, Pablo soon began making more complex compositions. His *Acrobat Family with Monkey* borders on an artistic joke. Pablo depicted the young parents gazing at their infant boy as though he were the object of traditional religious devotion. The reverent mood is shattered, however, by the equally fond gaze of a large ape who sits nearby. It's a strange painting. For art historians who are familiar with thousands of Madonna and Child paintings, the work seems to be a well-calculated paradox. Pablo almost certainly was inspired by his own studies in the Paris museums.

Paradox is also evident in the rose period's melancholy harlequins. They wear Napoleonic hats that seem completely out of place with their pink or red tights and ruff collars. Pablo also found paradox in depicting entertainers. Although their business was to excite people and make them laugh, in their private lives Pablo showed them listless and sad. The acrobats, who inspire awe in the circus tent, are shown by Pablo as quite ordinary people behind the scenes.

Early in 1904, Pablo showed his work with three other

artists in a Paris gallery. Apollinaire, his new friend, wrote a rave review, praising Pablo's talent, his combinations of horror and fantasy, of mysticism and delight. Several other reviewers praised the show. Most liked the rose pictures far more than the earlier blue paintings.

Pablo had already learned to read reviews with some skepticism. Apollinaire, after all, knew very little about art. But these particular reviews did encourage Pablo to expand the scope of his rose-period mood.

He began painting a wider range of carnival folk. Fat jesters, lithe dancers, clowns, and child acrobats appeared on his canvases. Pablo seemed to identify with these people. Like artists, they are exiles from normal life. They have no permanent homes. Always on the point of departure or arrival, they are life's wanderers. This seems to be their main cause of sadness. It is a sadness quite different from that of the blue period. Circus folk, after all, are wanderers by choice.

Thanks partly to the show and the early reviews, a few collectors began to take an interest in Picassos. In 1905, Wilhelm Uhde, a German collector who saw Pablo's work in a secondhand shop, asked to meet the artist. The shop owner sent Uhde to Pablo's favorite Montmartre café. There, Uhde soon was able to introduce himself to Pablo. The two became lifelong friends, and Uhde over the years built a valuable collection of Picassos.

The year 1905 was one of development for Pablo. Thanks largely to Fernande, he had become fluent in French. He took a keen interest in French literature, and he was able to expand his circle of friends. He met Gertrude Stein.

It was a lucky encounter for them both. A young American intellectual, she had been living in Paris since 1903. She had come to France to continue the study of psychology that she had begun at Johns Hopkins University, where she had recently earned a medical degree. As it turned out, she soon became interested in broader aspects of life—literature, art, and people.

Her two brothers were also living in Europe. Michael was a business genius who would continue to build the family's fortune, which was already substantial. Leo, an art collector, would introduce Gertrude to modern art.

One day, Leo went into a secondhand shop not far from Vollard's gallery, where he saw a painting of a thin, nude girl holding a basket of red flowers. The dealer wanted one hundred fifty francs (about thirty dollars), which Leo thought was too much. The next day, however, he returned with Gertrude. She liked everything about the picture except the girl's feet, which she thought were too large for the thin body. The dealer offered to eliminate the feet by cutting the canvas. But the Steins, refusing to consider the outrageous suggestion, bought the picture, big feet and all. In this way, the first Picasso entered the Stein collection.

They asked the shop owner to introduce them to the artist. The meeting was arranged, and Pablo soon faced two people who, in their strange way, would help him to fame and success. They were a memorable pair. Leo, a bearded giant, towered over everyone. Gertrude, whose stout figure was covered by a tentlike dress and whose feet sported Turkish slippers, wore her hair like a Russian countess, coiled on top of her head. She was no more self-conscious about her odd outfit than she was about her mannish manner.

Gertrude's instincts, combined perhaps with her training in psychology, told her immediately that Pablo was a man of strength, willpower, and independence. And she liked him. Perhaps she recognized some of her own stubborn traits. Pablo, who had never met anyone like the Steins, had trouble getting a conversation started. But he did let it be known, almost at once, that he wanted to paint Gertrude's portrait. She liked the idea and invited Pablo to her home on the rue de Fleurus.

6

THE STEINS

After Picasso became famous, Gertrude Stein loved to boast that it was she who discovered him. This angered Leo, who actually was the first in the family to appreciate Pablo's work, and it infuriated Pablo, who denied that he ever needed to be discovered.

Gertrude Stein, however, liked to stimulate her friends, and anger was sometimes a very effective form of stimulation. Referring to Pablo as "my little Napoleon" made him seethe. She also provoked him by saying that she had influenced his work.

Often during the many years of their friendship, Pablo avoided Gertrude for months on end. He always enjoyed repeating gossip about the Steins and was not above starting some gossip himself. But he and Gertrude would eventually patch things up, forgive everything, and become friends again. Pablo would return to rue de Fleurus.

On that first visit, Pablo brought Fernande with him. Although Gertrude was often ill at ease with pretty women, Fernande, who was candid and honest in her conversation, made a hit from the start.

There was another young painter at the Steins. He was a serious man who could easily be mistaken for a college professor. His name was Henri Matisse. He, too, was a genius, and, like Picasso, Matisse would soon begin building a reputation as one of the great innovators of modern art.

At the time of their meeting, Matisse had become interested in primitive art from Africa and the islands of the Pacific. He had started to collect African masks and undoubtedly discussed his interest with Pablo.

Matisse and Picasso, thanks to the Steins, were competitors from the day they met. Leo collected Matisses. Gertrude had decided to collect Picassos.

The rivalry between the two artists usually stayed on a friendly level. The two men had immense respect for each other. Although Pablo became famous for criticizing other contemporary artists behind their backs, even close friends, he was rarely heard to run down Matisse or his work.

The first visit to rue de Fleurus was followed in a few days by a gathering at Bateau-Lavoir. Pablo introduced Gertrude and Leo to Max Jacob, Apollinaire, and several other writers, poets, and artists, including some intense Spaniards. Gertrude was enchanted and invited everyone to rue de Fleurus. Gertrude soon began sitting for her portrait, but Pablo had unexpected trouble capturing his subject. Her personality, perhaps, was too complex.

Gertrude's Saturday-night parties were always stimulating. She invited artists, poets, reviewers, journalists, business leaders, politicians, generals, and all the expatriates she could find. The novelist Ernest Hemingway was a frequent visitor. Of course, Gertrude liked to say that she discovered him, too.

The walls at rue de Fleurus were covered with many contemporary paintings, including a growing number of Picassos. Gertrude was quick to instruct her guests on the merits of modern art in general and Picassos in particular. Her comments boosted Pablo's confidence, and her regular purchases of his work rescued him from poverty. But while he welcomed her support, he resisted her possessiveness.

Pablo's fascination with circus and carnival workers continued. One night, after visiting the circus with Max Jacob, Pablo painted a fat buffoon, whose ponderous body made a poignant contrast with his clown costume. It was another paradox. He did several of these heavy figures, sometimes including them in group scenes as a foil for the lithe acrobats and dancers.

This theme carried over into one of Pablo's early etchings. *Salome* shows the young dancer of biblical fame doing a high kick before a Herod who comes directly from Pablo's fat buffoon of the carnival paintings.

Among Pablo's new friends was a Dutch writer, Tom Schilperoort, who persuaded Pablo to accompany him on a brief visit to his home, a small town in Holland. Pablo could not afford to take Fernande with him. In fact, he had to borrow from Max Jacob to pay for his own train ticket. He packed a small bag. It was easy to pack his paints, but he had to snap the handles of his brushes in half to make them fit.

The Dutch women fascinated him more than the flat Dutch landscapes. Smiling, blonde, and healthy, the girls all seemed eager to pose for artists. Pablo soon decided that Nordic women were ideal models. He returned to Paris with several paintings of big, placid nudes. Fernande viewed them with displeasure, but the Nordic type would appear again and again in Picasso's work for the rest of his life.

While in Holland, Pablo became more concerned with precise anatomy. His bodies and his faces became more individualistic. He also took more care in the placement of his

Salome, *15 7/8″ × 13 3/4″, an early print, dating from 1905, reflects the happier spirit of Picasso's rose period. For the figure of Herod, he used one of the carnival figures that frequently appeared in paintings of this period.*

figures on the canvas. In the past, too, he had relied on outline to create his figures. Now he used light and dark surfaces to give his figures form and bulk.

Soon after his return from Holland, he stopped painting carnival scenes. Art historians now say that 1905 marked the end of Pablo's rose period. It must be remembered, however, that the term refers more to subject matter and mood than color. Picasso never gave up the rose tint completely. In fact, it remained a favorite for the rest of his career.

Before the year ended, Vollard, the agent who had refused to handle the depressing work of the blue period, began buying Pablo's recent paintings. His support, along with Gertrude's regular purchases, made life easier. Fernande and Pablo could eat in cafés more frequently.

Early in 1906, Pablo started doing portraits of other members of the Stein family. He did one of Leo with a rose background and another of Michael's son, Allen. But the portrait of Gertrude, begun soon after they met, caused great difficulty.

The first sitting was at Bateau-Lavoir, where Pablo made a quick sketch with brown and gray paints. Everyone but Pablo liked it. Gertrude's two brothers and several friends who saw it wanted the sketch left just as it was. Pablo insisted on trying again.

Gertrude returned to Bateau-Lavoir more than eighty times to sit for Pablo. He had little trouble capturing the flowing dark robe that Gertrude wore over her massive figure, but he could not solve the face. It was not a feminine face, but it was acutely sensitive. The harder Pablo worked at the problem, the more difficult it became. He needed a new approach, a new style, but it kept eluding him. Gertrude was patient and good-natured. She even laughed about the endless sittings, but to Pablo it was no joke. He had to solve the problem of this American friend's portrait.

Sometimes, instead of struggling at the easel, Pablo would

take Gertrude and her friends to a café or, better yet, to the circus. There, in a relaxed mood, he could study his subject. Back at the studio, however, he became tense again.

In the spring of 1906, Pablo ended a sitting by painting out his latest attempt at Gertrude's face. He put the unfinished canvas away. He had given up. Gertrude left Bateau-Lavoir puzzled and disappointed.

Pablo was exhausted. He had worked steadily for two years. It was time for a vacation, and at last, thanks to Gertrude and Vollard, he could afford to return to Spain in style. He and Fernande left for Barcelona in mid-May.

A proud Pablo introduced his French girlfriend to his family. The Four Cats had closed, but there were other cafés where he could show her off to his friends. Fernande, always in one of her big hats, loved the attention. Don José, however, clearly did not approve of mistresses. He said nothing, but Pablo felt the tension and soon became restless for a change.

Friends recommended Gosol, a mountain retreat some hundred miles west of Barcelona. It was a remote medieval town of nine hundred inhabitants. They moved into the town's only inn. The isolation was just what Pablo needed.

He filled a sketchbook with drawings, some of Fernande posing nude, others of the town. When he used color, the sketches showed the red ocher of Gosol's soil. His figures became sculptural. When drawing a face, for instance, he put more emphasis on the curved surfaces of the cheeks and the brow than he did on the outline of the nose or the mouth. He wanted elements of the face to have individual form and to look like three-dimensional parts of the whole.

Although the short painter and his tall mistress drew stares, Pablo felt comfortable with the people. In Paris, Pablo was often aloof, but in Gosol, Fernande was amazed at how quickly he became part of the community. His experience at Horta had given him an understanding of and appreciation for the Spanish peasant.

When not posing, Fernande studied English. Pablo drew. Ideas now came easily, and he was excited about a new style that seemed to be emerging. He recalled later that he felt at this time like a singer who was reaching for notes not yet written in the music.

Several things combined to influence the new style. Greek statues, which he had studied since his first days at art school, had certainly left an impression, but Pablo had recently seen primitive art, particularly a collection of bronze statues of the fourth and fifth centuries A.D., which had recently been unearthed in Spain. These statues were both figures and symbols. They appealed to Pablo's love of paradox. Although he would later deny it, Pablo also was undoubtedly influenced by the primitive statues and masks from Africa that had already begun to interest Henri Matisse and other collectors in Paris. Distortion gave the masks compelling power.

But the greatest influence behind Pablo's experimentation was Paul Cézanne. Cézanne believed that all things could be simplified to a few basic shapes—a cone, a box, a sphere, a cylinder. In a landscape, for instance, Cézanne would simplify a series of hills into sections of horizontal cylinders. His trees would be cones; his houses would be boxes topped by triangles. Cézanne gave his landscapes and still lifes depth and made them look real through an inspired use of color.

When painting an apple, for instance, Cézanne might use a warm red to bring the curved front close to the viewer. The edges might be green or blue, making them recede. The use of pure color, rather than shading, was revolutionary. Pablo was among the first to appreciate what Cézanne was trying to do.

Pablo's new style evolved very slowly. One big breakthrough came when he drew Fernande lying nude on the bed and gave her a primitive mask for a face. But he put this startling work aside to develop other ideas. It would be several months before nudes with masks appeared in his work again.

In August 1906, the Gosol vacation came to an abrupt end when the innkeeper's daughter fell sick with typhus. To avoid exposure, Pablo and Fernande fled at once to Paris.

A few days after his return, he summoned Gertrude Stein for yet another sitting. He worked only on the face, leaving the rest of the painting untouched. He now knew exactly what he wanted, and it took little time to finish the portrait that had so long troubled him. He used his new style. Gertrude's face became stiff, almost wooden, like a crude mask. The eyes, of unequal size, created a tension in keeping with her character. This, combined with the intensity of her stare, made the picture an excellent likeness, capturing personality as well as appearance. It was not flattering, but Gertrude seemed pleased and hung the painting in a prominent place at rue de Fleurus.

Meanwhile, a group of painters, headed by Henri Matisse, had caused a great stir in Paris by showing paintings that combined emotional use of color with free and imaginative composition. The style was loose and showed the influence of primitive art. The figures were not always anatomically correct. Landscapes and still lifes often lacked perspective. But the *fauves,* or wild beasts, as they were dubbed by critics, created pictures that were full of emotion. They compelled attention.

Pablo had met many of the fauves at rue de Fleurus. He liked most of their work. One of them, a strong, handsome man named Georges Braque, shared Matisse's fascination with primitive art, but he was also fascinated with Cézanne's work. Pablo and Braque had much in common.

Pablo had the opportunity to exhibit with the fauves, but

he turned it down. He feared that becoming part of an art movement would restrict his freedom. And at this moment, when his style was in transition, he needed freedom desperately.

Just the same, although he would not freely admit it, the fauves influenced him, particularly in their bold treatment of anatomy. And Braque became a major influence, too.

Pablo, however, was never generous in crediting other artists for their help or influence. He continued to deny that African masks had influenced him, even after both Matisse and Braque recalled showing Pablo their collections at this time.

Perhaps Pablo himself was not sure what was changing his style. Cézanne, however, was in his mind constantly.

During the winter of 1906–7, Pablo's figures became more geometric and angular than ever. His female nudes looked like wrestlers. Their power, not their charm, commanded attention. His colors combined the red ocher of Gosol with pale pastel shades, but he was more concerned now with form than color.

To darken an area of a canvas, he sometimes neglected color in favor of a series of dark stripes or crosshatches. The crude treatment gave the paintings a sense of urgency and power.

He did a self-portrait. It was no more flattering than the portrait of Gertrude Stein. His masklike face, however, had the electric energy of a prophet. Indeed, he was on the threshold of prophetic discovery.

7

>—<

CUBISM

In the spring of 1907, the studio at Bateau-Lavoir became cluttered with paintings of stiff, distorted female figures. They looked like wooden totems carved to scare off or perhaps attract evil.

The canvases were not likely to please Vollard or any other dealer, but Pablo was so deeply involved with these strange figures that he could not be concerned with the opinions of other people. For several weeks, he had been struggling with a large canvas depicting prostitutes in a brothel. At first there were men in it, a sailor and a student. The student was holding a skull.

The work started, it seems, with some symbolic message about love and death, but Pablo eventually painted over the two men and the skull, leaving five large nudes with challenging eyes. The angular bodies were painted with red ocher, the color that had dominated Pablo's canvases since his trip to Gosol. The figures seemed to be mounted on a stage.

Pablo made many sketches of the composition, and he changed the picture itself several times. Faces were reworked, poses shifted. Most of the changes tended to simplify the images. Arms and legs, even folds of curtains in the background, were reduced to geometric chunks. Cézanne would have been startled to see his ideas being carried to such extremes.

The faces gave Pablo the greatest difficulty. He finally gave two figures angular faces, painted in the same style he had used for Gertrude's portrait and his own self-portrait. Wide eyes stare at the viewer, but the eyes are not symmetrical. For the figure standing on the left, he used a similar style, but while most features are shown in profile, the single eye faces the viewer to create the puzzling distortion of a figure facing sideways but looking frontward. This harked back to the ancient Egyptian manner.

The two remaining figures on the right side of the canvas, one sitting with an awkward body twist and the other standing, have the strangest faces. They look like grotesque masks roughly carved from wood. Inspired certainly by primitive art, the faces have long, sweeping noses and crudely drawn eyes. They are shaded with quick parallel brush strokes. Pablo finished the painting with a bowl of fruit centered at the bottom of the canvas.

But was it finished? Pablo wasn't sure. He knew he wasn't satisfied with it, but the struggle of painting it had created a flood of new ideas. And Pablo was curious to see how his friends would react.

At first, Pablo called it *Avignon Brothel* after a well-known establishment in Barcelona. Later, he changed the name to *Les Demoiselles d'Avignon (The Young Ladies of Avignon)*. Nothing like it had ever been painted before.

Most of the few who saw it were shocked. Some close

friends thought the young Spaniard had gone mad. Word soon spread around Montmartre that Pablo had created a scandal. Fernande began getting sympathetic looks from shopkeepers.

At first, it seemed that the only friend who liked *Les Demoiselles* was Georges Braque. And rumor said that it had driven him mad with excitement. Braque, some said, had locked himself in his studio and was creating a painting that was even more outrageous. Actually, the picture brought Pablo and Braque closer together. Braque, who had already been composing pictures with fundamental shapes, immediately recognized Cézanne's influence, and Braque appreciated Pablo's courage.

Pablo, well aware of the public sensation *Les Demoiselles* would cause, had decided not to let it out of his studio. But he willingly showed it to visitors. Matisse was horrified, and, on his next visit to rue de Fleurus, he advised Gertrude Stein to stop collecting Picassos. Gertrude's enthusiasm did indeed cool for a time, but she soon began buying Pablo's works again. Matisse himself eventually modified his opinion.

Vollard did not like the painting and said so. Other dealers agreed, but there was one young dealer, recently arrived in Paris, who liked it and wanted to see everything else Pablo had done.

Daniel-Henry Kahnweiler had given up a family business in his native Germany to open a small gallery on rue Vignon. He planned to specialize in modern art and had already begun buying work by Gauguin and Cézanne.

Kahnweiler had heard about Picasso from Wilhelm Uhde, the German who had collected works from the blue period. Kahnweiler soon became a regular visitor at Bateau-Lavoir, and Pablo visited his small gallery and liked what he saw.

Kahnweiler was most interested in Pablo's recent work, and he recognized *Les Demoiselles d'Avignon* as an extremely

Les Demoiselles d'Avignon, *8' × 7'8", was completed in 1907. Although it was not shown publicly for several years, the work created a sensation among Pablo's artistic friends.*

important painting. It was mad but at the same time profound. Kahnweiler wanted to hang it in his shop, but Pablo claimed it was not yet finished. He did let Kahnweiler take some of the preparatory sketches. A few weeks later, after several more visits to Bateau-Lavoir, Kahnweiler gained enough trust to take several paintings to show in his gallery. Thus began a long and profitable business association and a long and turbulent friendship.

Kahnweiler's friendship came at an important time. Largely because of the cool reception Matisse and Gertrude had given *Les Demoiselles*, Pablo and Fernande, for the moment, had stopped going to rue de Fleurus. Several old friends, leery of the strange painting, no longer appeared at Bateau-Lavoir. Some of the neighbors also avoided the couple, but this was not entirely due to Pablo's strange painting.

At an impractical moment, Pablo and Fernande had gone to the local orphanage and adopted a child, a little girl. The venture was a failure. Neither Pablo nor Fernande was prepared for parenthood. They soon turned the girl over to a kindhearted neighbor. The episode did nothing to improve Pablo's popularity.

Without Kahnweiler's friendship, Pablo might have reverted to sad pictures. Kahnweiler's praise of Picasso's work was obviously genuine. He had complete faith in Pablo's judgment and talent. This became obvious when Kahnweiler brought two wealthy Russian collectors to Bateau-Lavoir. Both soon began buying Picassos. Without Kahnweiler's friendship, this Russian market for Picassos would not have developed.

Although finding buyers for Pablo's paintings was a great financial help, Kahnweiler's most important contribution at this time was the encouragement he gave Pablo to continue painting in his new style.

Georges Braque was also a source of encouragement. His role in Pablo's creative life steadily gained importance. A year younger than Pablo, Braque had grown up in Le Havre on the Atlantic Coast. He had been living in Montmartre since 1902, trying, like Pablo, to scratch out a living as an artist.

Although he had shown with the fauves, he soon became uncomfortable with the excesses of color, rough brushwork, and lack of technique that some of the others in the group advocated. Braque preferred moderation to excess. Most of the fauves were under the influence of van Gogh's emotional work. Braque was more interested in the rational work of Cézanne.

Braque had spent the summer of 1907 in L'Estaque, Cézanne's favorite district, doing landscapes in a bold adaptation of the master's style. He had broken down natural forms of trees, hills, and houses into geometric shapes, in much the same way that Pablo had broken down elements of the female nudes in *Les Demoiselles.*

It is still not certain how many ideas Braque and Picasso exchanged at this time. It was obvious to them, however, that they were both exploring the same territory. Although they visited each others' studios often, for the next several months Braque and Picasso worked independently on parallel courses.

In the summer of 1908, Pablo and Fernande, with a dog and a cat, went to La Rue-des-Bois, a small village north of Paris. They set up a studio and living quarters in an abandoned barn that still smelled of animals. It soon became just as cluttered and unkempt as the studio at Bateau-Lavoir.

Pablo painted all day and often far into the night. He continued to reconstruct nude forms, but he also tried the new style on landscapes. Although he relied on dark greens for his forest scenes, most pictures that summer continued to be dominated by the earthy reds that he had started using at Gosol.

Braque worked again in L'Estaque, where he continued

producing landscapes in the Cézanne manner. He also tried breaking down and reconstructing nude figures and still lifes. Some of his landscapes, painted with the same tans and greens favored by Cézanne, could be mistaken for Cézanne paintings, but in most cases Braque's geometric shapes are bolder and more obvious. Many other Braque paintings of this period actually look more like Picassos. And some of Pablo's 1908 paintings were beginning to look like Braques.

Back in Paris, Pablo decided not to show his new paintings. He wanted only to continue working without interruption from anyone, not even Fernande. He rented a small studio and buried himself in seclusion. Sometimes he did not appear at Bateau-Lavoir until dawn.

Feeling neglected, Fernande began an affair with another artist. If he noticed, Pablo was too absorbed in his work to care. Each canvas, instead of being an artistic work, had become a learning experience. The greatest successes were the canvases that taught him the most. Were they worth showing, he asked himself? Probably not.

Unlike Pablo, Braque returned from his summer's labors wanting some reaction. He submitted six of his L'Estaque canvases in the 1908 fauve show. To his dismay, all six were rejected. Kahnweiler, however, offered to take all the recent Braques that would fit in his small gallery.

Although his friends flocked to the opening of the Kahnweiler show to see his work, Braque did not get the public exposure he wanted. The few critics who went to Kahnweiler's were puzzled. One of them marveled at Braque's interest in reducing everything to diagrams and cubes.

Picking up on this, another critic coined the word "cubism." Thus the new style got a name. Neither Braque nor Picasso liked the word. They regarded themselves simply as artists searching for new ways to paint pictures. If the new style had to be classified, "reconstruction" would have been more descriptive of what they were doing.

Braque's Kahnweiler show stimulated Picasso. It also started several other young artists experimenting with the new style. There soon emerged a vigorous group of painters who did not mind calling themselves cubists. Under the leadership of Braque and Picasso, they would give the twentieth century a new look.

The new style, however, took a long time to develop, and it went through several phases.

In the summer of 1909, feeling a need once again for his native Spain, Pablo took Fernande to Horta, where ten years earlier he and Pallarés had spent an ideal vacation. Pallarés could not join them, but he used his connections to find rooms for them in the town's only inn.

Pablo painted landscapes with the earth colors he now loved. His *Reservoir at Horta* treats a mountain scene in the same exaggerated Cézanne style that Braque had developed the previous summer at L'Estaque. There were many other landscapes. Pablo now felt confident with the style, and he was comfortable with the people of Horta. In the evenings, he and Fernande played game after game of dominoes with the farmers in a local café, where a guitarist played the music Pablo loved.

When the news spread that he and Fernande were not legally married, two righteous residents stoned the windows of their inn. Pablo dashed into the street, angrily waving a revolver. When he calmed down, Pablo paid for the damage to the windows, and within a few days the incident was forgotten. Their money, however, was running low, and Fernande and Pablo had to return to Paris sooner than they had planned.

Fortunately, Kahnweiler had been busy. Thanks largely to sales of blue- and rose-period paintings, Pablo found himself with ample spending money. He decided to move. He had lived and worked at Bateau-Lavoir for five years. It was time for new surroundings. He and Fernande settled into a building at 11, boulevard de Clichy, not far from Place Pigalle, an area that would become famous for its nightlife.

The new home was more comfortable and had far more space. It was also in a more respectable neighborhood. It had a studio with large windows overlooking the wide street.

Pablo felt wealthy enough to hire a maid. She wore a spotless apron and knew how to cook his favorite dishes. Fernande felt uneasy. The new home was far too classy for the bohemian life they had been living. She wondered if she would ever see their friends again.

Pablo, however, was delighted. The new home represented a leap up the social ladder. Moving to boulevard de Clichy was his first tangible sign of success.

Kahnweiler deserved much of the credit. He had now found collectors for Pablo's work in Switzerland, Germany, and Russia. Meanwhile, several Paris businessmen had formed a modern art investment club. This group, which stayed active until the start of World War I, bought several Picassos.

Picasso's new studio soon became just as cluttered as the old one. Paintings by himself and others leaned against or hung on the wall. African masks hung everywhere. Pablo now bought every mask that caught his fancy. He also carried home scores of other, even stranger, objects. Discarded pots, pieces of rope, paper or cloth with strange patterns, and other objects made some corners of the studio look like junk heaps. There was even a bicycle seat. He could not say why he wanted it, but it might be useful someday.

The home had also become a menagerie. There were three cats, Frika, the dog, and Monina, a recently acquired monkey. Only the animals were allowed in the studio when he worked. The maid could not enter at any time, and Fernande could enter only with permission. Pablo slept late, but around noon, he locked himself in his studio and did not come out until evening. After dinner, he usually went back to the studio to work until early morning.

Some afternoons, he went to the Louvre, leaving Fernande at home, alone.

Pablo's relations with Gertrude Stein were back on a good footing, and almost every Saturday night, he and Fernande dined at rue de Fleurus. Gertrude was buying Picassos again, but she and Leo, the true art expert, had become estranged. Alice B. Toklas, a thin, delicate woman from San Francisco, had moved into Gertrude's home to become her lifelong companion.

Pablo flashed many a wink and made crude jokes about the relationship behind Gertrude's back, but he continued to enjoy Gertrude's hospitality and patronage. Gertrude hired Fernande to help teach Alice French.

On some visits, Pablo and Gertrude would talk far into the night about art, literature, politics, philosophy, and, of course, their friends. They enjoyed each other's company and stimulated each other tremendously. Pablo by now was a big attraction at Gertrude's parties. He was not always polite to other guests. He could be aloof and sullen, particularly when other painters were discussed. If a pretty girl were in the crowd, however, he would sparkle with wit and good cheer. Usually, he would try to make a brief attachment. Then it was Fernande's turn to be sullen.

Pablo saw Braque daily. Although Braque was more organized and more methodical than Pablo, both had questioning natures, and both were eagerly seeking new means of expression. Braque's landscapes from his summer at L'Estaque had been rejected by the fauves largely because of their subdued color and their emphasis on geometric form. He would not change to please the public, but just the same, he sometimes had doubts.

Pablo seemed to be the only friend who approved, and the

71

approval was obviously genuine because Pablo was following Braque's lead. They discussed their ideas endlessly. To save time walking back and forth, they decided to share the same studio. Each new work was discussed as an experiment, an attempt at expressing some new concept. They had no idea where it would all lead, but the experimental approach avoided the anguish of failure. If something did not work, they simply painted over the canvas and tried again. Both men had stacks of recycled canvases.

Their paintings of this period are very hard to tell apart, and, to complicate the problem, neither man, for a time, signed his work. They viewed their experiments as collaborations.

They agreed that the subject matter should be simple. A few objects on a table were adequate for a still life, and still lifes dominated this phase of their work.

Pablo, however, applied their technique to portraits. Vollard, Kahnweiler, Uhde, and Braque himself all sat for him. The results were remarkable—broken elements, fragments of figures are rebuilt into structures that are recognizable likenesses. Vollard, who was gradually being won over to the new style, said that a child of three recognized him from Pablo's portrait.

Braque's company stimulated Pablo tremendously, and he genuinely wanted Braque to share his happiness and enthusiasm. While it lasted, it may have been the warmest friendship Pablo ever enjoyed.

It was during this period that Pablo decided Braque should be married. That decision led to a very strange evening.

8

MA JOLIE

Max Jacob had a cousin who owned a Montmartre café. Pablo decided that the cousin's daughter would be the ideal wife for his friend Georges Braque. Braque apparently favored the union. All that was needed was the cousin's approval. This would take some diplomacy.

Pablo enlisted some members of the old gang and they, along with Jacob and, of course, Braque, prepared to make a formal call. To make the best impression possible, they agreed to rent evening clothes, complete with black hats and silk scarves.

Then they descended on the cousin and his family. The evening went well at first. The marriage was proposed and the father seemed to like the idea. He served a round of drinks to seal the contract. The drinks were tossed down very quickly, making it necessary to serve another round, and another.

The hour grew late, but Pablo and his friends continued drinking and talking. They talked too much and stayed too late. And they had drunk far too much. When they finally left, they were unable to sort out their rented hats, cloaks, and scarves from their host's wardrobe. As a result, they left wearing the entire contents of the cousin's closet.

To no one's surprise, the marriage contract became unsealed at the first light of dawn, and for several weeks, Max Jacob was on uneasy terms with his cousin. Pablo and his friends avoided Max's cousin for months.

Pablo, however, did not lose sight of the main goal. He soon introduced Braque to another candidate, a charming girl who fell in love with Braque and willingly married him. It was a happy, lifelong union.

For some time, the independent artists of Paris had held two shows a year, one in the spring and another in the fall. Pablo and Braque did not participate in these shows, but they did let Kahnweiler exhibit examples of each new phase of their work. At Kahnweiler's, most of the attention came from other artists. Critics either ignored cubism or ridiculed it.

Among the artists who went to Kahnweiler's shows regularly were several who tried to adopt the cubist style. Those who understood what Braque and Pablo were trying to do began producing successful canvases. Many others, however, simply produced poor copies of Braques or Picassos.

Many artists who didn't experiment with the new style were affected by cubism just the same. If nothing else, they benefited from the freedom to explore, a freedom that Picasso and Braque had pioneered.

Retaining artistic freedom was one reason the two did not exhibit in the independent shows. They did not want to be influenced by public opinion or critical reviews.

Braque returned to L'Estaque in the summer of 1910 to paint still lifes and figures. Pablo and Fernande went back to Spain. This time, after visiting family and friends in Barcelona, they took a dockside house at Cadaques, at the northeast tip of Spain.

Pablo spent part of the vacation working on etchings he had promised to illustrate Max Jacob's book of poetry, a book that Kahnweiler planned to publish. He also did several drawings of boats, some still lifes, and some landscapes. These were all done in traditional style, with no hint of cubism. It seems that he needed a vacation from cubism. It is also possible that he did not want to work on the new style without Braque's company.

Back in Paris, real support came from Kahnweiler, who encouraged a wealthy Austrian doctor to begin buying cubist paintings. The doctor bought many, including several Picassos, and he continued to buy until the start of World War I. One day, these would be valued as one of the world's most important cubist collections.

Thanks to the interest of wealthy buyers, cubism soon began to gain some snob appeal. The idea that only the elite, a chosen few, could appreciate it, helped Kahnweiler sell more than one cubist canvas. Neither Picasso nor Braque encouraged this notion. They painted for themselves and for each other. They were not trying to make their work obscure to the public, but if that's how things stood, then too bad.

They enjoyed the confusion that arose over their unsigned pictures. When asked which of them had done a certain canvas, they would usually shrug and say it did not matter.

During the winter of 1910–11, Braque and Pablo were as close as they ever would become. Both became fascinated with aviation, which was then in its infancy. When not painting, they studied aerodynamics, went to air shows, and built model planes and gliders. Pablo began calling Braque "Wilbur Wright." Their friendship was so close that they tended to exclude others. Pablo's relationship with Max Jacob cooled. Max annoyed Pablo by continually talking about the poverty they had shared in Paris in 1903. For his part, Pablo would tease Max about his religion. The poet, born Jewish, had recently converted to Catholicism. He talked and wrote about his new faith endlessly.

Braque and Picasso took their experiments through three phases. The first, Cézannesque cubism, was typified by Braque's early landscapes at L'Estaque and Picasso's landscapes at Horta. These basically were extensions of Cézanne's theory that all elements of a picture could be reduced to a few simple geometric shapes.

In the next phase, called analytic cubism, the shapes lost their simplicity. Pablo's portraits of Kahnweiler and Uhde were typical of early work in this phase. Later, there was so little to recognize in his pictures that one could determine the subject only from the painting's title. Pablo's *Man with Guitar,* painted in the fall of 1910, looks nothing like a man or a guitar. There are just a few short, parallel lines, which an imaginative eye might see as the frets of a guitar. His *Accordionist* was mistaken back in Paris for a landscape. In the summer of 1911, Pablo gradually began returning to reality.

When Pablo and Braque returned to their Paris studio in the fall of 1911, they decided to include more recognizable objects in their pictures. This brought on the third phase.

Sometimes they painted in the object, but usually they simply glued it to the canvas and painted around it and sometimes over it. They used ticket stubs, bottle labels, newspaper clippings, or anything else that caught their eye. This style, which became known as synthetic cubism, often relied on the pasteup or collage technique, a technique that Braque and Picasso made respectable.

In 1911, Pablo had a solo show in Alfred Stieglitz's Photo

Session Gallery in New York City. Two magazine articles and brief notices of the show in the American press launched Pablo's reputation as an international artist. It was a small beginning, but it was important. Stieglitz, who would one day marry Georgia O'Keeffe, was the first influential American to appreciate the young European artists.

In the fall of 1911, Paris police appeared at Pablo's studio with a summons. He was to appear before a judge and explain how two bronze heads, missing from the Louvre's collection of early Spanish art, had come into his possession.

Pablo had a hard time convincing the judge he was innocent. Some two or three years earlier, Apollinaire had introduced Pablo to a collector who, unknown to them both, was a thief. Picasso said he had bought the bronzes from the man without the slightest suspicion that they had been stolen.

The judge was skeptical. Even today, it is hard to believe Pablo's protests. He was thoroughly familiar with the Louvre's collection of primitive art, particularly the Spanish work. He must have guessed that the heads had been stolen. Meanwhile, Apollinaire, who had received a third head from the thief, complicated the case by telling a conflicting story.

Apollinaire was charged with complicity in the theft and of heading a gang of art thieves. Actually, he was probably closer to being innocent than Pablo, but Pablo was not charged. He was simply told to go home and wait for further questioning.

Nothing happened. The charges against Apollinaire were eventually dropped. The police did not question Pablo again. But the experience terrified him. For the rest of the year, he dodged the police. He even bypassed police stations on his walks through the city.

Pablo rented studio space back at Bateau-Lavoir and tried to work there daily. There were many distractions. And he had other worries.

Fernande was restless. She had never felt at home on boulevard de Clichy. Pablo had been unfaithful several times with other women, but when Fernande saw other men, Pablo protested like a dying bull. Fernande thought he had no right to protest. She did not understand Pablo's jealous nature.

It was time for a change. It came early in the spring of 1912. Fernande moved out of the apartment and her friend, Eva Gouel, also known as Marcelle Humbert, moved in. It was all done so quietly that weeks passed before most of Pablo's friends realized a change had occurred.

Eva, who had been the mistress of Louis Markus, a Polish artist, was as frail and delicate as Fernande was healthy and robust. Four years younger than Pablo, Eva wanted security and respectability. She had grown to hate the bohemian life. She liked a well-ordered household. She even kept a family budget, something Fernande never considered. Pablo called Eva *ma jolie* ("my pretty one") and once painted these words on a cubist still life. Although he never painted her portrait, Pablo would write PABLO AND EVA, PRETTY EVA, or I LOVE EVA on other canvases of the period.

Lettering was an important part of the synthetic phase of cubism. It provided more real or recognizable elements to contrast with the abstract fragments. Braque was apparently the first to make bold use of letters in a picture of a man seen through a café window, a window that bore the name of the café.

Because of his personal worries, Pablo's productivity

Recognizable forms almost disappeared during the height of Pablo's cubist period. Although this 1912 work is called Woman with a Guitar, *the figure is only faintly suggested. The painting, 39³/₈" × 25³/₄", is also called* Ma Jolie.

COLLECTION, THE MUSEUM OF MODERN ART, NY
ACQUIRED THROUGH THE LILLIE P. BLISS BEQUEST

slumped during the winter of 1911–12, but as soon as he took up with Eva, his creative energy returned. He felt himself launched on a new life. He asked Kahnweiler to find him a new apartment. Meanwhile, he and Eva headed for a summer vacation at Ceret in the Pyrenees Mountains, not far from Spain. To Pablo's dismay, Fernande was there with friends who scolded him for abandoning her without financial support. After a few angry scenes, Pablo took Eva to a resort near Avignon in southern France, where the Braques were vacationing.

In Avignon, Pablo and Braque launched a full collaboration on the final phase of cubism. Pablo found a piece of oilcloth that was printed to look like the woven caning of a chair seat. He pasted it onto an oval canvas and incorporated it in a still life. He included lettering in the picture and, for the final real element, gave *Still Life with Chair Caning* a frame made of rope. This was a bold combination of collage and painting, which introduced recognizable objects in an abstract reconstruction.

A little later, Braque found a shop in Avignon that sold a variety of wallpaper printed with imitation wood textures. He used three strips of this paper, along with the words "bar" and "ale" on an oil still life he called *Compote Bowl and Glass.* Soon both artists were using collage in almost all their work.

Meanwhile, Kahnweiler was working hard to build Pablo's international reputation. Several Picassos from the blue and rose periods had been shown in Barcelona earlier in the year, to great acclaim. The show established Pablo as the hometown hero who had found fame in the world of art. His work was also shown in London, Moscow, Berlin, Cologne, and Munich. Reactions were mixed. In London, one critic decried Picasso's "perverted talent." The German critics, however, were generally more enthusiastic.

It was Pablo's habit to grumble against all art dealers. Just the same, he signed an agreement with Kahnweiler, making him his sole agent for all recent work for the next three years.

Knowing Pablo wanted to make a big change in his living arrangements, Kahnweiler found an apartment for the artist and his new mistress in Montparnasse, on the other side of the river Seine from Montmartre. The new address at 242, boulevard Raspail was more in keeping with Eva's desire for respectability.

They moved in April of 1913, but before Pablo could settle down in the new home, he received distressing news from Barcelona. Don José was dead. Pablo and his father had never reconciled their differences on art or life-styles. Deeply depressed, Pablo left for the funeral. Don José, now famous only as Pablo's father, had found little happiness. Pablo blamed himself for both his father's unhappiness and his death. He arrived in Barcelona in such anguish that he had difficulty speaking to his mother or his sister.

Back in Paris, he faced more trouble. Eva, who had always been frail, was suffering from a sore throat and a chronic cough. Pablo decided that the mountain air and warm climate of Ceret would help them both. Max Jacob went with Pablo and Eva, and the Braques soon followed. Unfortunately, it rained steadily. Eva continued to cough.

Pablo worked on the illustrations for another of Max Jacob's books and also turned out several cubist collages. He and Eva returned briefly to Paris in June. Her health remained poor, however, and they promptly went back to Ceret. There Pablo fell ill. The event made news. His health was discussed in all the Paris journals and several other European newspapers. For Pablo it was a surprising discovery. At the age of thirty-one, he was being treated as an important artist, a celebrity.

9

WORLD WAR

Modern art came to America early in 1913, and the United States was not prepared. Americans still viewed the impressionists and the postimpressionists with suspicion. How could they appreciate the fauves and the cubists?

Alfred Stieglitz had been the only American bold enough to show the works of Matisse, Picasso, and a few other twentieth-century Europeans in his Photo Session Gallery. Now Stieglitz took a real chance helping to promote a major show of modern art in New York's armory. With much public fanfare, the show opened in February 1913.

The public outcry could be heard from coast to coast. The show countered everything the American public knew about art. The critics judged landscapes by their realism, still lifes by the careful brushwork, and portraits by their likeness to the subject. The fragmented works by Braque, Picasso, and the other cubists confused, shocked, and outraged the American viewers.

The public outcry, of course, was the best possible publicity. People crowded into the armory by the thousands. Artists came from all across the country. The show had a tremendous influence on American art and American tastes.

Most artists were fascinated. Many drew inspiration from the bold and fearless works. Even those who reacted against the show conceded that the Europeans had introduced a new and broader approach to art, an approach that had to be respected.

The show established Paris as the art capital of the world. Europeans already knew this, but now Americans understood that Paris was the place to be for art collectors and art students. Matisse, Braque, and Picasso lived and worked in Paris. From now until the middle of the century, Americans would take the lead from Paris.

Pablo and his contemporaries were not fully aware at the time of the armory show's impact. In the spring of 1913, Pablo and Eva moved from boulevard Raspail to a larger studio-apartment. Pablo worked steadily. Most evenings they stayed home. When they did go to a café, they saw many more Montparnasse businessmen than artists. Probably because of Eva's frail health, they stopped attending Gertrude Stein's Saturday-night parties.

Despite their quiet life, Eva's health did not improve. Finally, doctors concluded that she had tuberculosis. Although medicine was making great strides against the disease, it had long been considered fatal. In Eva's case, there seemed to be little hope.

Pablo worked harder than ever. His reconstructions took on more varied color. He continued to experiment with collages, using newspaper clippings, pieces of cloth, labels, and anything else that caught his imaginative eye. Often he would paint so that the work looked like a collage or else use collage in such a way that it looked like a pure painting. These playful illusions added a new and delightful dimension to synthetic cubism.

He relied more on simple silhouettes to suggest an object and less on internal form and shading.

He drew a cubist portrait of Apollinaire, to be used as the frontispiece in the poet's latest book. The picture was Pablo's way of getting even. The poet liked to see recognizable images in art. For this reason, he had praised the works of artists whom Pablo had grown to detest.

Pablo's portrait of Apollinaire was a jumble of fragments. They were skillfully composed, but the picture did not contain one recognizable shape or image. The poet, to everyone's amusement, was forced to use the picture. It was not the last time Pablo and his friends would make fun of Apollinaire. But despite Pablo's barbs and the poet's artistic ignorance, he and Pablo remained on good terms.

Early in 1914, the Paris businessmen who had been investing in modern art for several years decided to liquidate all their holdings. The auction, set for March 2, was expected to test cubism and other modern trends against the art market. The foes of modernism were convinced that the auction would bring such poor prices that the modern movement would evaporate. The moderns themselves, on the other hand, believed that here at last was a sale that would show their real value. Collectors, dealers, and artists themselves from both sides of the controversy waited for the auction with high expectations.

There were only two cubist painting up for sale, but the *fauves* were well represented, as was Picasso's rose period. In all, twelve of his works were going on the block. He did not attend the auction, but almost all of his friends joined the crowd.

Modern artists, it soon became clear, were going to make

news. A Matisse still life sold for 5,000 francs, or about $1,000. Other fauve paintings did not sell for such high prices, but then the Picassos went on the block. The first went for 1,100 francs, or $220. A fair beginning. Then his *Girl Singing* was knocked down for 2,100 francs, or $420. Better! Next, *Three Dutch Girls,* which Pablo had painted on cardboard during his trip to Holland, sold for 5,200 francs, or $1,040. Terrific!

But it wasn't over. *The Tumblers* was big, eighty-nine by ninety-three inches. The owner was reluctant to sell it, but there was no wall in his house big enough for it. There were several collectors at the auction, however, who saw the size as an asset. The price went up and up. Finally, the bidding stopped at 11,500 francs, or $2,300.

The price was unheard of for a modern work by a living painter. Kahnweiler ran out of the auction room to deliver the news to Pablo. The artists would receive 20 percent of the sales, and for this reason alone, the news was very welcome at Pablo's studio. But for Kahnweiler, the big news was that the auction had erased all doubt. Pablo Picasso was the leading painter of Paris. And he was still young, just thirty-three years old. Kahnweiler's instincts had not failed him. Now, both he and Pablo could look forward to a very promising future.

Europe, however, was tumbling toward chaos. The worst war the world had ever experienced loomed on the horizon. Everyone knew it was coming, but they did not know how to stop it. While factories built arms day and night, statesmen made feeble efforts to preserve peace.

Pablo's French friends prepared to be mobilized in the army. Pablo, as a citizen of Spain, was not obliged to fight, and he had no intention of volunteering. He was not about to let a war interfere with his art.

He spent hours and hours in his studio. His collages followed a natural trend into three-dimensional art. Instead of using pieces of paper or cloth, he glued scraps of metal or wood on flat surfaces. He retained the reconstruction style of cubism; in fact, the three-dimensional pieces emphasized it, but he was no longer painting. It was sculpting. He continued making cubist sculptures at Avignon, where he and Eva spent the summer of 1914. Braque was also there, but he was too distracted by the impending war to do much work.

War began on August 2. That same day, Pablo and Braque said good-bye to each other on the platform of the Avignon train station. Pablo suffered a terrible feeling of loss as the train pulled away carrying his friend to war. Braque, though seriously wounded, would survive the war, but the friendship the two men enjoyed was lost forever. Pablo liked to say later that after that day at the railroad station, he never saw Braque again. It was Pablo's dramatic way of saying a friendship had died.

Cubism also died in the war. It would revive with peace, but it would come back in too many different styles to have the same influence it had had in the early years.

In the first months of war, Pablo seemed to be the only artist in France who went on painting. Without Braque, however, he lost interest for the moment in cubism. He explored other styles.

He and Eva did not return to Paris until November. The city was dead. All their friends, it seemed, had gone to war. Kahnweiler, in Rome at the start of the war, could not return to Paris because he was still a German citizen. If he went back to Germany, he would be forced to fight against France, a country he loved. He could be safe only in a neutral country. Meanwhile, the French government, acting under the alien property law, confiscated his valuable collection of paintings and drawings. His gallery was closed.

It was a lonely time. Pablo was acutely uncomfortable in public. The cafés were filled with men in uniform. People glared at him in his civilian clothes. Why wasn't he fighting?

Not a student of politics, he did not fully understand the causes of the war. He knew he was against it, and he called himself a pacifist. For the patriotic French, however, "pacifist" was simply another word for shirker or coward.

Pablo and Eva spent their evenings at home for weeks on end. The only evenings Pablo spent away from the apartment were when he went out to take Russian lessons from a friend. Eva tried to hide the gravity of her illness. She developed the fear that Pablo would leave her if he knew she was dying. Pablo, however, needed Eva's company and support more than ever before.

His moods were more unpredictable than ever. Some evenings he could be silent for hours at a time. On other occasions he might talk incessantly. He would boast. He would be humble. He tried not to talk about the war, but it was impossible. Most of his friends were in it. When on leave, they visited him and described it. It was horrible. People were losing their limbs, their eyesight, or their sanity. Some were dying.

It was hard to work. Many of the paintings of this period had the geometric forms of cubism, but they became more decorative and colorful than anything he had done before. Was this the right way to turn? Without reactions from Braque and Kahnweiler, he could not be sure. Even Gertrude Stein could not help. She had left on vacation before the war and had not yet returned to Paris.

He tried to divert himself with watercolors and pencil drawings. But he still worried about the war and about Eva's illness, which seemed to grow worse every day.

In May of 1915, Braque was carried from the front with a serious head injury. He spent months in various hospitals in and around Paris. Pablo never wrote to him or went to see him.

Eva was too sick in the summer of 1915 to leave Paris.

Eventually, she had to be hospitalized. Pablo was devastated. All through the autumn months, he watched her grow weaker and weaker. Finally, on December 14, 1915, she died.

This was one of the lowest points in Pablo's life.

Without Jean Cocteau, Pablo might have gone into total seclusion. Pablo had met this ambitious young gadfly, full of poetry and gossip, just a few days before Eva's death. Cocteau, extremely responsive to the moods of other people, sensed Pablo's suffering and appreciated the isolation he must face.

Some friends who were away at the war claimed later that Cocteau took advantage of Pablo's loneliness and used the artist to further his own ambitions. But Cocteau did not rush his friendship. He genuinely idolized Pablo, and they met at a time when Pablo desperately needed to be idolized.

Two months passed after Eva's death before Cocteau called on Pablo. He came wearing a harlequin's costume under his raincoat. He expected Pablo to paint his portrait. It was impossible not to catch Cocteau's high spirits. On that visit Pablo did not paint the portrait. He simply listened with delight to Cocteau's endless chatter.

His connections, particularly in the theater and the ballet, seemed endless. He also knew the leaders of Paris society. Cocteau's world was far from the bohemian Paris that Pablo knew, but this was just as well. Pablo wanted to escape from the past.

Cocteau represented an escape. And he soon began sug-

In his final phase of cubism, Pablo used more contrast and brighter colors. In Harlequin, *72¼" × 41⅜", done late in 1915, the figure, though highly abstract, is still recognizable.*

COLLECTION, THE MUSEUM OF MODERN ART, NY
ACQUIRED THROUGH THE LILLIE P. BLISS BEQUEST

gesting a challenge. It was time to bring modern art to the theater. Why didn't Pablo try his hand at designing ballet sets and costumes? Pablo liked the idea at once. Here was a way to reach a new audience, a way to broaden his influence. Pablo and Cocteau spent hours discussing their ideas.

Pablo, however, was still fighting depression. Early in 1916, he moved from his apartment, and all its memories, to Montrouge, a cheerless suburb on the south side of Paris. There, renting a small house at 22, rue Victor-Hugo, he soon made friends with an interesting neighbor. The composer, Erik Satie, whose music was as new and strange to the public as Pablo's art, spent many evenings with Pablo. Satie believed the time had come to bring contemporary music to the ballet. For this, of course, he won the support of Cocteau.

Pablo did some cubist constructions, but he also returned to realistic drawings and paintings. Even Don José might have approved of his traditional style. He sketched portraits of Max Jacob, Cocteau, and several other friends. There were now many new friends.

When Gertrude Stein finally returned to Paris, Pablo introduced her to Satie and once again became a regular guest at rue de Fleurus on Saturday nights. He brought a procession of pretty girls, some of whom had grand social connections. The girls roused Gertrude's jealousy. She feared the loss of Pablo's friendship.

Pablo was broadening his Paris connections far beyond Gertrude's intellectual circle, but this was thanks to Cocteau, not the pretty girls.

Cocteau introduced Pablo to Serge Diaghilev, the bold and energetic leader of the Ballets Russes. Diaghilev had brought such modern composers as Stravinsky, Ravel, and Debussy to the ballet. He was not afraid to experiment, and he had come to Paris to discuss Cocteau's scheme for modern sets and costumes.

Designs for the Ballets Russes had been dominated too

Pablo, in front of one of his cubist abstractions, glares at the camera in this 1916 studio photo. RÉUNION DES MUSÉES NATIONAUX

long by the stiff traditions of Russian art. Diaghilev was getting ready to stage a new ballet. It was called *Parade*. The script was by Jean Cocteau. The music was by Erik Satie. Why not have sets and costumes by Pablo Picasso?

Pablo said no.

Cocteau was shocked. Diaghilev was confused. Pablo suspected by now that Cocteau was using him to gain friends and influence in the art world, and he did not trust Cocteau's artistic judgment. The poet had recently organized a combination art show and music recital. Fully aware of culture's appeal to the social set and able to capitalize on it, Cocteau turned a large studio into a gallery music hall and promoted the show avidly throughout Paris. Picasso reluctantly agreed to participate in Cocteau's "lyre and palette" production. His paintings were hung with those of Matisse, Amedeo Modigliani, and other moderns.

The show was a success. It provided a rare diversion for war-weary Paris. Cocteau's friends, however, seemed to be far more interested in the Spaniard and his intense, dark eyes than in anything Pablo had painted. He did not consider them a serious audience.

It was with this in mind that Pablo said no to *Parade*. Cocteau used all his energy to bring Pablo into the production. Diaghilev, Satie, Cocteau, and Pablo had several long meetings. The poet's enthusiasm was infectious. Pablo knew he was being used, but finally, on condition that he be given full artistic control, he said yes.

He had begun a new adventure.

10

OLGA KHOKLOVA

Pablo began exercising his rights as artistic director at once.

Parade was about a street carnival. Its characters were acrobats, clowns, and all the other show people Pablo had observed and painted since almost the start of his career. Cocteau had created these characters in a romantic, sentimental vein. Pablo wanted them to be as real as he could make them.

Cocteau protested, but Pablo made change after change in the script. The music that Satie had written for the dancers was punctuated with sirens, train horns, clacking typewriters, and the roar of motors. Pablo told Cocteau that the music required real characters.

In the end, Pablo practically rewrote the entire script. Satie sided with Pablo on most of the changes, and although they met daily with Cocteau, some changes were made behind his back.

Cocteau was beside himself, but short of canceling the production, there was nothing he could do.

Meanwhile, Pablo was inventing costumes that were far more modern than Diaghilev or Cocteau had dreamed. The cast included three "managers" who were to run the carnival and introduce the acts. Pablo dehumanized these characters beneath cubist constructions of wood and cardboard. Cocteau referred to the costumes as "human sets."

Pablo put one of the show's street magicians in a cubist costume of red, black, yellow, and white spirals and crosshatches. In a more traditional vein, he put the acrobats in tights streaked with blue flame.

To confuse everyone, Pablo's preliminary drawings for the curtain could only be described as classical. Diaghilev and most of his staff were disappointed and said so. Their reaction had no effect on Pablo.

He went to Rome, where *Parade* was being rehearsed in February 1917. The Italian artists known as futurists welcomed Pablo as an old friend and showed him around the ancient city, but he was much more interested in discussing current work than ancient ruins.

Pablo soon devoted full time to the rehearsals, wanting to make sure that Diaghilev understood and appreciated all the changes that had been made. Cocteau, distracted by the male dancers, now dropped his protests and even supported many of Pablo's ideas. In his free time, Pablo drew portraits of some of the dancers and members of the staff. He met the composer Igor Stravinsky and drew his portrait. The ballerinas, of course, were his distraction, but he did his best to focus full energy on the stage setting and costumes.

He drew more sketches for the curtain. He prepared the final designs for the set and costumes. These drawings he

In Rome in 1917, Pablo courted ballet dancer Olga Khoklova, whom he later married. Here the couple is seen with Jean Cocteau.

RÉUNION DES MUSÉES NATIONAUX

would carry back to Paris, where everything would be made under his supervision.

Meanwhile, he had noticed a bronze-haired ballerina. She was not a star. She had freckles and she was shy. At the same time, she was very strong willed. Her character appealed to Pablo's love of paradox. Olga Khoklova, daughter of a Russian colonel, was ten years younger than Pablo. She had been in Diaghilev's troupe for several years, long enough to know that she would never get any lead roles. Her career was at a standstill. She was ready to consider marriage. Pablo represented security, fame, and a rise in social stature.

Diaghilev warned Pablo about Russian women. They regarded a dinner date or any other kind of rendezvous as part of courtship, and courtship in Russia was a one-way road to marriage.

The warning did no good. Pablo was in love. He followed Olga about like a puppy. He went with her to Naples and Florence, where the troupe performed several other ballets before going to Paris for the final work on *Parade.*

The theater work was so absorbing that the war seemed remote to most members of the troupe. For the love-struck Pablo, busy day and night, the war seemed very far away. The fighting, however, was now taking a terrible toll on human life and spirit. Diaghilev, too, was out of touch with the reality of the war. Had he known the public mood, he would not have offered an experimental ballet.

Paris was practically a military zone. Trench fighting took lives, without an advantage to either side. Both sides were exhausted. Although the United States joined the Allies on April 6, 1917, substantial help could not be expected for several months. Mutinies had broken out in the French army. At home, civilians stood in line for rationed food and fuel and complained.

Russia, an ally at the start of the war, had withdrawn when revolt overthrew the czar and brought in a new regime. Many French citizens regarded Russians as traitors. Even though members of the Ballets Russes were refugees who had fled from the new regime, they were still regarded with suspicion by many Parisians.

Cocteau, always sensitive to public mood, promoted the show as a benefit for war victims. This seemed to solve the problem. The Châtelet, where *Parade* was being staged, was sold out weeks before opening night. But some had bought tickets in order to make trouble. These included people with anticubist as well as anti-Russian sentiments.

Parade opened on the evening of May 18, 1917. The theater crowd was well dressed and, before the curtain rose, well behaved. Many of Cocteau's society friends had come to support the poet. Many others in the crowd, however, had come to attack modern art. They were prepared.

In another time or another place, the premiere of *Parade* might have been received with acclaim. Instead, there was trouble from the start. The first cubist costume was greeted with shouts, catcalls, and police whistles. Those trying to hush the disturbance only added to the din. The emotional Parisians soon became physical.

Men swung their fists; women clubbed and poked with their fans. The shouts, whistles, and cursing drowned out the music. Some angry patrons departed.

Meanwhile, the show went on. A little girl, a major figure in the show, did a ragtime dance to music no one could hear. A magician, who swallowed an egg and made it appear again in his shoe, was ignored. The noise subsided a bit when two dancers in a horse costume did their routine, but as soon as a manager appeared in cubist costume, the roar of protest erupted again. The dance continued, but there was no way to restore order.

Diaghilev was delighted. He had built his reputation on controversy. *Parade* was an event that would be the talk of Paris for months to come.

As expected, the critics were unanimous in their condemnation, but friends showered Cocteau, Satie, and Pablo with praise. Serious fans of ballet saw *Parade* as a successful experiment, a new form of theater. Pablo took both praise and criticism with a shrug. In the dreary months of war, attention of any kind for an artist was welcome. He knew that his entry into the theater broadened his reputation as an innovative artist. He wanted to do more work with ballet. The time and motion of performance were new dimensions for his art.

When the Ballets Russes went to Barcelona on tour, Pablo followed. Although he stayed at his mother's apartment, he spent most of his time with Olga. He enjoyed showing her off to old friends, and he wanted all the dancers to see the

Barcelona he knew and loved. It was a homecoming for Pablo, and it brought him back to a more realistic style of art.

Olga probably also influenced his work at this time. She did not understand or appreciate modern art; she rated work by its realism. Pablo did more realistic work. He painted a view of city rooftops, trees, and streets in the style of the impressionists. But he also did portraits of Olga that were as bold and colorful as any Matisse painting. Occasionally he returned to cubism. It was never a problem for Pablo to switch abruptly from one style to another. In fact, it seemed to stimulate him.

Olga influenced his behavior as well. He surprised his old friends by wearing a dark suit, bow tie, pocket handkerchief, and watch chain. He carried a cane. Amused friends who remembered his bohemian past agreed that he looked like a clothing-store model.

Pablo, who had the daily use of a friend's studio, decided to remain in Barcelona when the ballet went on to Madrid. Old friends, now unanimous in their respect, honored him with a banquet on the night of July 12.

The ballet returned to Barcelona, gave a production of *Parade,* and then went to Paris. There Olga resigned from the troupe, telling everyone that she was giving up her career to marry Pablo. The wedding, however, was delayed. There were many things to be done and decided.

Early in 1918, Pablo and Matisse had a joint show in Galerie Paul Guillaume. It was a good experience for both artists. Their respect for each other was growing rapidly. They traded pictures. It was something Pablo had already started to do with other artists he admired.

Meanwhile, Olga declared that the small house in Mont-rouge was not suitable for married life. She would live there temporarily, but Pablo must promise a large home in a more respectable neighborhood. She also insisted on a maid and a carriage.

Although Pablo agreed to these demands, he began to ignore Olga's artistic advice. To her distress, Pablo concentrated on cubism. He did many still lifes with guitars, glasses, fruit dishes, and other familiar images of the synthetic period. He also did some realistic work and made some playful animals from bent wire, a departure that would eventually lead to major sculpture.

Finally, in late spring of 1918, Pablo and Olga found an apartment in Hôtel Lutétia, a rather ugly building on Paris's Left Bank. Pablo retained the Montrouge cottage for storage and occasionally for work. The new apartment, however, had a large studio, and Pablo did most of his work there.

He saw few old friends. Gertrude Stein and Alice Toklas were in the south of France, nursing wounded Americans. Most artist friends were either still at the front, wounded, or dead. Those not in the service were far too bohemian for Olga.

They did see Apollinaire frequently. He had recovered enough from his head wound to be married. The ceremony took place on May 12. Exactly two months later, in a long Russian Orthodox ceremony, Pablo and Olga were married. Later they repeated their vows before a judge in a simple civil ceremony.

A new life had begun for Pablo.

On November 9, 1918, Guillaume Apollinaire died of complications from his war wound. Two days later, the armistice ending the war was signed. Of the two events, the death of his friend moved Pablo more than the return to peace.

Apollinaire had represented Pablo's bohemian days, his long struggle for recognition, his crazy, youthful whims and ambitions. Thinking of Apollinaire reminded Pablo of cheap cafés, cluttered studios, and the haunting faces of Montmartre. The poet's death brought a kind of death to Pablo's past.

Life was changing. Peace brought changes, but it was Olga who did the most to take Pablo away from his old life and his old friends. Shortly after Apollinaire's funeral, Olga and Pablo moved to 23, rue la Boétie in a classy neighborhood of Paris. It was a neighborhood where sloppy clothes and long hair would cause people to stare. No bohemian artist could feel comfortable on rue la Boétie. Max Jacob, already terrified of Olga, rarely called. Braque, out of the hospital at last, also kept his distance.

Jean Cocteau, however, was always welcome. Olga appreciated Cocteau's social connections and his gossip about the Paris elite. Olga also encouraged visits from Léonce Rosenberg, the art dealer who also had social connections. During the war, Rosenberg had begun selling Picassos. Rosenberg's brother, Paul, operated a posh art gallery next door to the Picassos' new home.

Receptions in the gallery attracted the social-conscious crowd that Olga loved. The Rosenberg brothers had well-established international outlets for art. Thanks largely to them, Picassos began to appear in museums around the world.

But Pablo often treated his dealers badly. At one time, he suspected Léonce Rosenberg of cheating him on purchases, but even after Kahnweiler returned to Paris, Pablo continued to sell to Rosenberg. Sometimes he managed to get Kahnweiler and the Rosenbergs bidding against each other for pictures. He would use these same tactics on other dealers.

Kahnweiler, Pablo's most loyal supporter, struggled to get reestablished after the war, but he did not get much help from Pablo. More than once, Pablo accused Kahnweiler of cheating, but the agent understood and appreciated Pablo better than anyone else. He remained faithful, despite all difficulties. Gradually, he put his business back together.

The Picassos occupied two floors of their building. The upper floor became a studio as cluttered and messy as any before. There were cigarette butts on the floor and unframed paintings by Matisse, Cézanne, and others on the walls. The maid was not allowed to clean the studio. Olga never entered.

She remained on the lower floor, where all was clean and orderly—a middle-class apartment furnished in middle-class taste. Only a few paintings gave any hint of the genius upstairs.

Olga gave parties for her friends. Pablo did not seem to mind that his friends were never invited. Perhaps he thought it was time for a break with the past. Things were changing.

The art world was in a turmoil. Cubism was no longer controversial. A new movement, dadaism, which had emerged as a protest against war, turned into a protest against all artistic tradition. It attracted the most public attention and outrage. Dada's leading practitioners produced photos decorated with paint, pieces of metal and paper sandwiched between glass, and found objects mounted on pedestals.

At one dada exhibit, there was a bicycle wheel mounted on a wooden stool. Later, a urinal was exhibited as a work of art. These were defiant acts, but they forced people to adjust their definitions of art.

Pablo was fascinated, but he did not join the dada artists or exhibit with them. They did influence him. Later, using found objects, Pablo would create some profound, sometimes funny art.

While dada was beginning, however, Pablo worked hard in other styles, many other styles. One day, he might do a cubist still life, the next day, a realistic portrait, and the next, figures in the classical tradition. Thanks to his growing reputation, there was little difficulty in selling any of his work. He was growing wealthy and famous.

101

Picasso was uneasy with success. This may be why he changed styles so often during the first few years after the war. He was glad, though, to continue his contacts with the theater. Diaghilev wanted sets and costumes for a production of *The Three-Cornered Hat*. The music had been written by Spanish composer Manuel de Falla. Pablo worked very hard to make the show a success. It opened in London to rave reviews on July 22, 1919.

Pablo and Olga, who went to London for the opening, stayed three months, attending parties and receiving honors. During this period, Pablo turned out scores of sketches and finished drawings. Some of his studies for the sets and costumes of *The Three-Cornered Hat* were published that fall by Paul Rosenberg.

Later, when the ballet premiered in Paris, a banquet was given to honor Pablo and de Falla. Pablo, in black evening dress and red sash, found himself surrounded by admiring ladies in beautiful gowns. He loved the attention, but he insisted that all honors should go to de Falla, a fellow Spaniard.

Soon after this episode, Pablo began focusing on a classical style. He seemed to be searching for new interpretations of what he had learned in school. He produced balanced compositions in pleasing, almost bland, colors with well-proportioned, if somewhat hefty, figures, usually female dancers or bathers. Some of them, clad in loose robes or togas suggesting Greek or Roman times, led collectors to call this phase Pablo's antique period. Although his sources were unmistakable, the style was unmistakably Picasso.

11

MARRIED LIFE

The cubist fans who had been loyal to Pablo were dismayed by his return to classical work. He seemed to be rebelling against modern art. Most critics, however, generally welcomed the new style. One critic theorized that cubism had been a necessary evil, a phase Picasso had had to go through in order to develop a higher form of expression. The classical Picassos were also welcomed as a happy and reassuring contrast to the wild creations of dada.

A few critics, however, were suspicious. They warned that the classical works were just eyewash, intended to prepare the way for further outrages.

Pablo ignored the critics and gave no explanations. He undoubtedly painted classical pictures because he felt the need to paint them. He may have thought for a time that he had exhausted cubism. But he soon returned to it. For the

103

moment, the classic style was a way of starting over, to see what might emerge from the old traditions.

He had long admired Jean Ingres, a realistic French painter who had carried classical traditions into the nineteenth century. Pablo studied Ingres's careful draftsmanship and used the same care in his own work. Greek and Etruscan art and the Roman art of Pompeii were also strong influences at this time.

Of course, Pablo did not simply copy old pictures. His classical figures have a bulky, three-dimensional quality that make them distinctly his. Soon he played with greater distortion. Some of his bathers began to look like wrestlers. His big women with big muscles seemed to be poking fun at tradition. And in the middle of this development, he occasionally gave the Rosenbergs or Kahnweiler some new cubist paintings. It sometimes seemed that he wanted to confuse his critics.

Diaghilev asked Pablo to design another ballet. *Pulcinella,* based on the burlesque figure of the hook-nosed clown Punchinella, would have many other characters from the tradition of the comic theater. Music would be by Igor Stravinsky, a composer Pablo knew and admired.

With great enthusiasm, Pablo threw himself into the project. The action, he decided, would take place on a pure white apron at the front of the stage. The white made a startling contrast with the blue and gray background and the colorful costumes of the dancers. Pablo insisted that the apron must have a fresh coat of white paint after every performance.

After several delays and much debate over both the music and the costumes, the premiere was staged in Paris on May 15, 1920. It was a great hit.

Soon after the premiere, Pablo and Olga headed south for a vacation on the French Riviera. They rented a summer home in Juan-les-Pins, a coastal village east of Cannes. He worked in several styles, turning out a series of still lifes, some landscapes, and several giant nudes or bathers. Monumental with impassive features, the figures looked like female gods.

Pablo used a similar style to paint large, pregnant women. His inspiration was Olga. She was pregnant, and Pablo was delighted. He had earlier painted "maternities" in his blue period, but those figures had been thin and sad. Now the women were robust and proud.

It was a happy summer for Pablo. The marriage seemed to be a success, and he was working. He returned home with scores of new canvases. He promised himself a return visit to the Riviera.

Soon after the Picassos returned to Paris, Max Jacob was hit by a carriage. He spent several days in a hospital, where Pablo visited him regularly. Their friendship, however, had become strained. Pablo's success emphasized Max's poverty and caused embarrassment. Eventually, after regaining his health, Jacob moved to a home in the country, and Pablo heard from him only rarely. This pleased Olga, who had never liked Max.

Olga may have caused yet another temporary estrangement with Gertrude Stein. Gertrude and Pablo argued, but later neither of them could remember what the argument had been about.

The relationship between Pablo and Kahnweiler also became strained at this time. Kahnweiler had recently opened a new gallery not far from Pablo's home. Pablo was not a frequent visitor, and Kahnweiler delayed collecting new Picassos for his gallery until 1923.

Postwar art in France lacked the controversy of the early years. Braque and a few others continued painting cubist still lifes, but cubism no longer outraged anyone. Matisse, who had moved to the south of France, was doing figures, decorative interiors, views from his windows and his balcony, and charming still lifes. He outraged no one. The dadaists caused plenty of controversy among other artists, but the general public took little interest.

Olga gave birth to a boy on February 4, 1921. They named him Paul, which was soon converted to Paulo. Pablo took his role as father very seriously. Despite his affairs with other women, he had strong family feelings, and he loved children.

In the spring, modern art received another test on the Paris market when the French government auctioned off two collections it had confiscated during the war under the alien property act. First, the works belonging to the German collector Wilhelm Uhde went on sale, and then those in Kahnweiler's prewar collection. Foes of cubism and other traditionalists were dismayed when the Uhde auction took in almost three times more than the amount expected. Buyers came from around the world.

Kahnweiler's collection was huge. It included 118 Braques and 132 Picassos. The volume forced the prices down, making it possible for Kahnweiler to buy back some of his favorite works. Young collectors were also able to make purchases. Despite the lower prices, the interest and the vigorous bidding at both sales proved that cubism was far from dead. For the moment, its critics fell silent.

Meanwhile, prices for current Picassos rose steadily. Rosenberg asked for and received eighty thousand to one hundred thousand francs (sixteen thousand to twenty thousand dollars) for recent Picassos.

Pablo cut Juan Gris, a fellow Spaniard, out of a job with the Ballets Russes in the spring of 1921. Gris was originally selected to design *Cuadro flamenco,* a ballet based on Spanish dances. Unfortunately, Gris was too ill to get to Monte Carlo, where the Ballets Russes was based, as soon as Diaghilev expected. By April, however, he had recovered enough to report for work. There was still ample time for him to do the job.

When he arrived in Monte Carlo, however, he discovered that Pablo had replaced him. Diaghilev gave no explanation, but Gris later discovered that Picasso had earlier written Diaghilev to say that Gris was too sick to consider the job, but that he, Pablo, would be happy to design *Cuadro flamenco.*

Gris returned to Paris more sad than angry. Later the ballet failed in both London and Paris.

Instead of returning to the Riviera in the summer of 1921, Pablo rented a villa at Fontainebleau outside Paris. He used Olga and Paulo as models in domestic scenes, but most of his energy was devoted to landscapes, bathers, giant nudes, classical figures, still lifes, and portraits. He also made a stunning return to cubism, doing two versions of *Three Musicians.* These were large, colorful canvases, each showing three men seated with their instruments. He made the pictures look like decorative collages, with the bold shapes of the compositions looking like paper cutouts, but everything was painted. Pablo was using an illusion he and Braque had developed during the synthetic phase of cubism.

His energy was amazing. He worked quickly and steadily and still found time for his family and a few of Olga's parties.

His remarkable productivity continued into 1922. In addition to his usual output of paintings, he illustrated two books, including Cocteau's latest collection of poems. Olga, perhaps jealous of Pablo's long hours in the studio, wanted more attention. Pablo was not always sympathetic. He and Olga argued occasionally, but they had no serious disagreements at this time.

In the summer of 1922, they went to Dinard, an Atlantic beach resort in Brittany. He painted cubist still lifes, realistic portraits of Paulo, seascapes, and more nudes and bathers. His cubist work was becoming more colorful, with more solid shapes. The "broken-glass" effect was gone. His bathers lost some weight. They were now more delicate, graceful, and feminine.

In September, Olga suddenly fell ill and had to be rushed to Paris for an operation. She recovered rapidly, and Pablo returned to Dinard to bring back Paulo, who had been left with a nurse.

After the failure of *Cuadro flamenco,* Pablo lost some of his enthusiasm for the theater, but Cocteau persuaded him to design the set for Sophocles' *Antigone.* As the opening night approached, however, Cocteau grew very nervous. Pablo had done nothing. The actors rehearsed on a bare stage. Cocteau pleaded for action. Finally, two days before the opening, Pablo came to the theater and calmly handed Cocteau a crumpled piece of paper. Pablo said it was the model for the set. Cocteau thought he was joking.

Before Cocteau's eyes, however, and before the startled eyes of the actors, Pablo hung a backdrop of crumpled blue canvas. The stage at once became a dark cavern. He then rubbed the canvas with a stick of red pigment to create the texture of marble. The realism was breathtaking. Next, with a few brush strokes of dark ink, he created three Doric columns to mark the cavern entrance. The actors and the stagehands broke into applause. Pablo had worked magic. Later, Pablo confessed to Cocteau that the columns had been an afterthought.

Pablo vacationed with his family on the Riviera at Cap d'Antibes, not far from Juan-les-Pins, the summer of 1923. He invited his mother to join them. It was Doña Maria's first visit to France. She loved it.

Gertrude Stein, who visited the vacationing Picassos, reported that she and Doña Maria sat on the beach watching Paulo play. Although they shared no common language, they seemed to understand each other perfectly in their praise of

Pablo. Working with continued intensity, Pablo's cubism became even more colorful at Cap d'Antibes.

About this time, *The Arts,* an important New York magazine, printed a Picasso interview, "Picasso Speaks," which was widely circulated.

Meanwhile, Pablo began work on the set and costumes for another ballet. For *Mercure,* with music by Satie, Pablo composed a set out of shapes braced by wire frames. Stagehands were trained to move these colorful shapes in time to Satie's music. Unfortunately, the moving set drew attention away from the dancers. Paris audiences booed. Even the show's producer, Count Cyril Beaumont, conceded that the whole idea was silly.

By 1925, Pablo had returned to painting harlequins and clowns in a realistic style reminiscent of his rose period. Paulo posed for him in a harlequin costume. Pablo's interest in the bullring as a theme for pictures and drawings also returned. Images of bulls, dead horses, and horses being gored by bulls filled his notebooks. For the most part, however, there was little violence in this period of Pablo's work. He was at peace, a proud father, and about as content a husband as he could hope to be.

Relations with Cocteau had cooled somewhat. Pablo no longer needed Cocteau to maintain his contact with the Ballets Russes. He gave Diaghilev a drop curtain depicting two women running on a beach. It was first used in the ballet *Le Train Bleu,* but Diaghilev liked it so much he used it in all his future ballets.

In 1925, the Picassos spent several weeks in Monte Carlo, headquarters of the Ballets Russes. Olga enjoyed the company of the dancers, and Pablo needed to discuss future productions with Diaghilev.

It was at about this time that *Les Demoiselles d'Avignon* was sold for twenty-five thousand francs (about five thousand dollars). For years, the canvas that had been such a touchstone for cubism had remained rolled up in a dark corner of Pablo's studio. But now it was wanted along with everything else created by his hand. Pablo was a little sad to part with it, but he knew he could always return to that style.

And this, in a way, is what he did. Large paintings with distorted figures began to take his full interest and energy. The colors were different and the shapes more distorted than they were in the 1907 work. Limbs and torsos looked like rough shapes torn out of paper.

Dance, painted at Monte Carlo, shows three figures drawn with a childlike disregard for reality. They dance before an open window and balcony. The background, with large areas of darkness, diagonal and vertical lines for shading, and patterns suggesting wallpaper, recalled synthetic cubism. But the positions and the distortions of the dancing forms made the picture more dynamic than most earlier works.

The painting pointed the way toward yet another style.

12

MARIE-THERESE

After a productive summer at Juan-les-Pins with Olga and Paulo, Pablo returned to Paris.

Olga had stopped hiding her dislike of Pablo's friends. She also had stopped holding her temper. It could be violent. She attacked Kahnweiler as a cheat. She raged at Pablo's lack of attention and accused him of being unfaithful. Their arguments grew nasty.

Olga's behavior influenced Pablo's mood and his work. He alternated between fits of rage and long periods of silence. He painted women with threatening teeth and wild eyes. Then these demons would abruptly give way to gentle figures with soft curves and smiles.

To take his mind off domestic troubles, he made several trips to Barcelona to visit his mother and sister and his old friends. On one of these trips, he met a thin, young artist whose work impressed him greatly. Salvador Dalí would find fame as a surrealist, but at the moment he was unknown. Pablo tried to put his work in Paul Rosenberg's hands. Rosenberg was interested, but Dalí wasn't.

In January of 1926, Pablo met Christian Zervos, a young Greek who had just published a scholarly book on Greek art, emphasizing works that earlier art historians had ignored. The book was controversial and successful. He had also started a new magazine called *Cahiers d'Art (Art Notebooks)*.

Pablo and Zervos became lifelong friends. Zervos's repeated praise of Pablo in his magazine compelled the art world to look to Picasso as a leader. Eventually Zervos began building a catalogue of all Picasso's works. This became almost a full-time project. Zervos was still adding to it when he died in 1970.

In 1926, Pablo painted *The Milliner's Workshop*, which used contrasting shapes, linked by a complexity of swirling lines, to suggest workers at their tables. It carried on many of the techniques of cubism, but the geometric shapes, particularly those depicting faces, were playfully interlocked, and the interior suggested a stage, reflecting Pablo's work with the ballet.

He had been playing with interlocking features since painting *Dance* the year before. Now he carried the style into portraits, overlaying the frontal view of a face with a hard-edged profile. This simultaneous or double view was to become common, almost a trademark, in many of Pablo's later works.

He also continued to paint female monsters, treating them now as if they were huge statues on a beach with backgrounds of limitless, surrealistic space. He treated limbs and torsos like twisted, deformed structures. The powerful, frightening, often hateful women were the product of what had become a very unhappy marriage. Pablo would continue painting these creatures for several years to come.

Pablo's troubled marriage probably influenced such 1930 works as Seated Bather, *64¼" × 51". While the imagery delighted the surrealists, Pablo was not willing to adopt the restrictions of their movement.*

COLLECTION, THE MUSEUM OF MODERN ART, NY

MRS. SIMON GUGGENHEIM FUND

Despite their growing marital difficulties, Pablo took Olga and Paulo to Juan-les-Pins for the customary summer vacation. Once again, it was a working vacation. He returned to Paris with many new paintings and drawings.

The monstrous females now dominated his work. They grew more hateful as his troubles with Olga increased. The tortured figures had recognizable hands, feet, breasts, and eyes, but the figures were inhuman.

Pablo had begun having affairs with other women. They were brief, but early in 1927, he saw a young blonde with bluish gray eyes and a well-formed, athletic figure. She reminded him of the Dutch girls who had been such willing models back in 1905. Pablo saw her in front of a department store on a busy Paris street. He followed her and eventually went up and spoke to her. He said she had an interesting face and he would like to paint it.

"Who are you?" she asked.

"I'm Picasso."

The name meant nothing to Marie-Thérèse Walter, but she was young, just seventeen, and she was curious. She agreed to sit for Pablo. Thus began the longest of his many love affairs.

Marie-Thérèse was very much alive, healthy, and even tempered. She had an immediate influence on Pablo's art. Although he continued to paint his monsters, he also did many portraits of healthy, blonde women. Limbs and features were sometimes distorted in these pictures, but there was nothing frightening or hateful about them. They glorified the female form and stressed Pablo's virility.

Visage (Face), 8″ × 5½″, a 1928 lithograph, is thought to be a portrait of Marie-Thérèse Walter, who had become Pablo's mistress a year earlier.

COLLECTION, THE MUSEUM OF MODERN ART, NY
GIFT OF MRS. JOHN D. ROCKEFELLER

Pablo, not hinting that there was another woman, asked Olga for a divorce. She went into a violent rage. Pablo dropped the idea. Marie-Thérèse said there was no purpose in making a change as long as she and Pablo were happy.

For several summers, Pablo put Marie-Thérèse up in an apartment near his vacation home. He spent as much time with her as he did with Olga, but he was discreet enough to keep the affair a secret from his wife. Many of his friends were not aware of Marie-Thérèse's existence at this time.

Despite domestic complications, his work continued with the same remarkable energy and inventiveness. However, the public was not always appreciative.

Although prices for modern paintings had increased steadily since the war, there was in some quarters a growing reaction against such art. Right-wing newspapers and magazines equated modern art with communism and other dangerous influences. Anti-Semites credited the Jews with all the outrages of modern art. One very influential reactionary wrote that Picasso was a hoax. One article said Picasso invented the picture without a top or a bottom. In the United States, the Hearst papers echoed the reactionary tirade.

Pablo paid little attention to most of the barbs, but he was amused to learn that teachers at the San Fernando Academy in Madrid, where he had once studied, were careful not to mention his name. It was ironic that, after thirty years, the school's most famous living student was not appreciated by its faculty.

Pablo resented the attitude of the French government. Despite his growing fame, no French museum had acquired a Picasso painting. The government continued to ignore Picasso until 1950, when a museum finally bought one of his works.

In the years between wars, Pablo's energy alone was enough to merit recognition. In addition to painting, often at the rate of two canvases a day, he produced scores of

116

etchings and book illustrations. He rarely turned down a job. When the young Swiss, Albert Skira, came to him saying simply that he wanted to be a publisher, Pablo was sympathetic. Skira had not even decided what to publish when Pablo agreed to work with him. They finally decided on a new edition of Ovid's *Metamorphoses,* a work neither Skira nor Pablo had read.

While Pablo and his family were vacationing at Cannes in July 1927, Paul Rosenberg staged a Picasso show in Paris. The successful show added to Pablo's reputation and boosted his prices. Soon after he returned to Paris, his *Harlequin Family,* a rose-period gouache (opaque watercolor) work sold for 52,000 francs (about $10,500), an unheard-of price for a work on paper by a modern painter.

The financial crash of 1929 was a disaster for most painters and dealers. The Rosenberg brothers suffered heavy losses. But even during the darkest years of the depression, Picassos continued to sell at substantial prices.

Pablo's international reputation, despite an often hostile press, grew and grew. In 1931, while a New York gallery was showing his more abstract paintings, a London gallery staged "Thirty Years of Pablo Picasso." In 1932, there were again two major Picasso shows, one in Paris and the other in Zurich, Switzerland. The Paris show, covering thirty years of work, was made up of 236 drawings, watercolors, and oils. Most critics, still blinded by tradition, did not approve. The variety of styles was astounding. One critic stated that what might be said correctly for one group of paintings would be completely wrong for another. It was hard to write about Picasso without contradicting oneself.

But collectors knew what they wanted. Works of the blue period, once shunned by most galleries, were now in demand. *Blind Man,* one of these early works, was acquired for Spain's Toledo Museum at a cost of 110,000 francs ($22,000).

Ambroise Vollard, who had refused to handle some of

Pablo's early work, was now eager to have Picassos in his gallery. Pablo, who had stayed on good terms with Vollard, let him replace the financially troubled Rosenbergs as a major dealer in Picassos.

In 1930, Vollard proposed an ambitious plan. If Pablo would do one hundred etchings and engravings, Vollard would publish them. The order could not have been filled in a lifetime by some artists, but Pablo completed the assignment in six years. Roger Lacourière's workshop handled all the printing, but every plate was engraved or etched by Pablo himself. And while he worked on the plates, he was also turning out paintings, drawings, and book illustrations in remarkable volume.

The *Vollard Suite*, as the hundred-print collection became known, is one of Picasso's major legacies. The images and styles cover a wide range, representing Pablo's broad interest and versatility. Forty-six plates follow the theme of the sculptor in his studio, usually with a model. Fifteen plates depict a minotaur, the half-man, half-bull monster of Greek mythology. Four are studies of Rembrandt, the famous seventeenth-century Dutch artist. Five are rape scenes, three are portraits of Vollard, and twenty-seven are of unrelated subjects.

While working on the Vollard project, Pablo also renewed his interest in sculpture. This explains his many prints of the sculptor's studio. Most of them show the artist working with his female model, a nude, of course. Often both are depicted looking at a bust or an abstract sculpture. The studio prints represent Pablo's first major investigation of the creative process. They introduced a theme that would be repeated again and again during the rest of his long career.

The minotaur would also appear again. It combined the bullfight heritage with Pablo's love of antiquity. The bull represented chaos and the man represented civilization. The minotaur, half man and half bull, was thus another paradox.

Painter and Model, *a 51 ⅛″ × 64 ¼″ painting done in 1928, was an early exploration of a theme that would fascinate Pablo throughout the rest of his long life.*

For Pablo, the bull also represented his own sexual appetite. It is a wonder during this period that he found any time for work. While seeing Marie-Thérèse Walter regularly, Pablo also carried on countless affairs with other women. He lived with Olga, but there was no hope for the marriage. Divorce, however, was no longer discussed. There was Paulo to think of, and Pablo was, after all, a Catholic. Olga would not even consider a divorce.

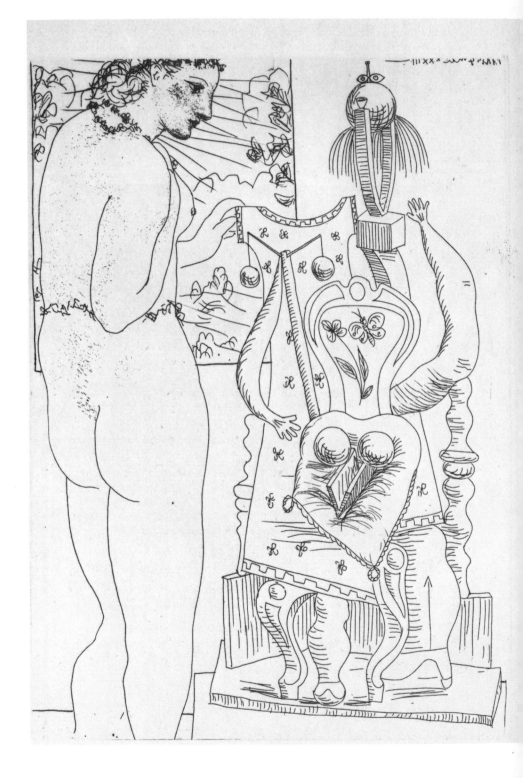

If anything, Pablo's sexual appetite increased with age. In the fall of 1931, he turned fifty, and, as if to prove he was not losing his youth, he increased his adventures with women. His fame helped attract them. Friends marveled that he was rarely seen in public more than two or three times with the same woman. Marie-Thérèse, installed in an apartment at 44, rue la Boétie, not far from his own home and studio, did not go out with him. He still did not want Olga and his friends to know about Marie-Thérèse.

In 1931, Pablo bought a villa west of Paris. Château de Boisgeloup proved to be an ideal retreat. He built a large studio there and soon filled it with sculpting tools, metal, clay, and heaps of found scrap. He provided comfortable living arrangements for Olga, but she rarely visited Boisgeloup.

Pablo also bought an Hispano-Suiza, a large and expensive car, and he hired a uniformed chauffeur to drive it. Although Pablo often entertained friends at Boisgeloup, his only regular companion at the château was Spanish sculptor Julio González. It was González who taught Pablo how to weld, but more often than not, Pablo was the teacher and González the student. Sometimes Pablo and Julio stayed at Boisgeloup several days at a time, but normally Pablo had himself driven back to the city late each evening.

Pablo had been commissioned to create a monument for Apollinaire. He and González discussed the project endlessly and made countless models for the statue. Several years would pass, however, before a statue was placed on the poet's

This 1933 etching, Model and Surrealist Sculpture, *10⁹/₁₆″ × 7⁵/₈″, says a great deal about Pablo's sense of humor and the unlimited range of his artistic style.*

COLLECTION, THE MUSEUM OF MODERN ART, NY
ABBY ALDRICH ROCKEFELLER FUND

grave, and it was the work of another artist. One casting of the monument Pablo designed finally found a place in New York's Museum of Modern Art; another is in Paris.

Most of his other sculpture from this period had its source in primitive art. From small pieces of wood, he carved long-limbed figures with little heads. He also made plaster models for huge heads, some more than two yards high. They had big noses and heavy features. Others were inspired by Marie-Thérèse. Meanwhile, he played with found objects, creating sculpture out of nuts, bolts, auto parts, kitchen pots, and wire.

Sometimes Christian Zervos organized parties on the château porch. The Braques, González, Kahnweiler, and Kahnweiler's brother-in-law, Michel Leiris, were regular guests. Pablo was now able to see all the old friends whom Olga had refused to entertain.

Pablo no longer attended Olga's parties at rue la Boétie, nor would he wear the business suits she had once insisted on. Their meetings almost always turned into loud arguments. Olga screamed. Pablo steamed. He later told friends that he had lost patience on one occasion and ended the discussion by dragging Olga through their apartment by her hair.

Gertrude Stein had begun to write her memoirs, disguising them under the title *The Autobiography of Alice B. Toklas.* She wanted Pablo to hear what she had written about the artist's early days in Montmartre, the studio at Bateau-Lavoir, and Fernande. Pablo brought Olga with him when he came to Gertrude's house for the reading. Gertrude, of course, did not read far into her account before Fernande's name came up. Olga immediately jumped to her feet and marched out of the house.

Pablo wanted to let her go, but Gertrude insisted that he try to find her and bring her back. Olga, however, had fled, and for many months she refused to see Gertrude, the person who had insulted her honor.

Critics are still talking about the symbolism that Pablo loaded into a 1935 etching, **Minotauromachy,** *19½" × 27⁷/₁₆". It seems that the young girl, armed with innocence, is the only one not running from the frightful beast.*

The first issue of the magazine *Minotaure,* founded by Albert Skira, with one of Pablo's monsters on the cover, was issued in 1933. It carried an article on Picasso's sculptures. In the same year, the first of many catalogues on Pablo's graphics was published.

Although Pablo welcomed this publicity, there was another publication he tried to suppress. Fernande had written her memoirs, and three chapters of the book had appeared in a magazine. Publication of the full book, however, was delayed, undoubtedly because of Pablo's threats of a lawsuit.

It turned out, when the book was finally published in abridged form in 1933, that Fernande had been discreet in her memory of the days at Bateau-Lavoir and rather kind to Pablo.

Pablo was not so kind to Fernande. She was poor most of her life. Pablo could easily have helped her, but he did nothing until several years later, when she became seriously ill.

In August of 1933, Pablo, Olga, and Paulo, now twelve, visited Barcelona briefly. Pablo hungered for his native land. Spain was having serious political difficulties. Landowners and church and military leaders, reacting against the country's reform-minded republic, threatened to overthrow the government. Pablo had always remained aloof from politics, but he seemed to sense that profound changes were coming. He wanted to see the country once again before it was too late.

Thus, in 1934, from August through September, he and Olga visited San Sebastian, Burgos, Toledo, Sargossa, Madrid, Barcelona, and many small towns and villages in between. They both may have hoped the trip would repair their marriage, but when they returned to Paris, their relationship had worsened. Pablo, in fact, was too upset to work.

Finally, in the summer of 1935, Olga moved out, taking Paulo with her. She did not go far. Her hotel was just around the corner from her former home. Almost daily, she wrote nagging letters to Pablo. There was again some talk of divorce. Pablo said he dropped the idea because the property division would be too complex, but, like most Spaniards, Pablo regarded divorce as disgrace. This was a strong but unspoken consideration.

Marie-Thérèse, meanwhile, had become pregnant and moved to the outskirts of Paris to stay with her mother. The baby was due in October 1935.

With Olga and Marie-Thérèse gone, Pablo found rue la Boétie a lonely place. He wrote to his old friend the Spanish writer Jaime Sabartés, who had recently returned to Europe after a career in journalism in South America. Pablo asked him to come to Paris and be his business manager. Sabartés, who had not found much success himself, was ready to live with someone who had. Furthermore, his admiration for Pablo was as strong as ever.

He agreed to Pablo's suggestion and prepared to move into the apartment.

On October 5, 1935, Marie-Thérèse gave birth to a girl. It was her idea to name it María de la Concepción, after Pablo's sister who had died at the age of four. The name was soon shortened to Maya.

Pablo loved playing the father's role. When Marie-Thérèse moved back to Paris, he spent many spare hours caring for the baby, watching her sleep, even changing diapers. Maya would giggle with laughter when Pablo played with her.

Marie-Thérèse did little laughing at this time. Normally a cheerful person, she now wanted Pablo to get a divorce and marry her. Pablo refused. The tears flowed.

13

GUERNICA

Jaime Sabartés arrived in Paris on November 12, 1935, and settled at once into the apartment at rue la Boétie. He arrived at a difficult time for Pablo. The break with Olga had upset him so much that he was unable to paint, but he still had the need for self-expression. He started writing poetry.

He took his poetry very seriously, and Sabartés, a serious poet himself, helped and encouraged Pablo.

The old friends talked for hours. Their conversations often went far into the night. Sabartés, who lacked Pablo's great energy, had trouble staying awake, but he knew Pablo had a desperate need to talk.

They had much to talk about. Pablo and Jaime had not seen each other for twenty years.

Although Pablo did not go out at night for several weeks,

he eventually began visiting Montmartre cafés, places Pablo and Jaime had haunted during their first years in Paris. Jaime tired early and the cigarette smoke irritated his weak eyes, but he would stay with Pablo until after midnight when the cafés closed.

Pablo ignored Sabartés's discomfort. Back at rue la Boétie, the weary poet would go to bed, while Pablo would go walking with the dog, Elft.

A difficult friend at any time, Pablo was now especially irritable over his inability to paint. He began to blame Sabartés for his problems. He cursed and shouted at the poet.

Sabartés calmly organized the household. One of his main chores was to serve as gatekeeper for Pablo. There were specific times when friends could visit, and then there were specific friends who could visit. The job gave Jaime a feeling of importance. He loved authority. Soon Pablo's friends realized that they must stay on good terms with Jaime.

Pablo's poetry was strange stuff. Like Gertrude Stein, Pablo made little or no use of punctuation. He separated his thoughts with dashes. Eventually, he even did away with spaces between words. His poems became a sort of code that only he could decipher.

Jaime praised the work, but Gertrude told Pablo he should stick to painting. Pablo, believing Gertrude felt threatened by his literary talents, once again became a rare visitor at rue de Fleurus.

Pablo's friendship with Paul Éluard strengthened at this time. Éluard, himself a sensitive poet, was genuinely interested in Pablo's writing and saw it as another dimension of Pablo's genius.

Like Pablo, Éluard had been married to a Russian. She had left him for Salvador Dalí, the Spanish surrealist. Trying to get over this domestic disaster, Éluard took a seven-month journey around the world. After he returned to France, he joined the Communist party. Although Pablo, until now, had had little interest in politics, Éluard's commitment to communism impressed him greatly.

Éluard had remarried. Maria Benz, nicknamed Nush, had been a circus performer. She was clever and entertaining—always excellent company when Pablo and the Éluards got together.

With Olga's departure, Marie-Thérèse had become more possessive. Pablo, who once used her as an escape from his marriage, now wanted an escape from Marie-Thérèse. Early in January 1936, while in a noisy café with Jaime, he found a new woman.

She had dark eyes and dark hair, and she was seated at another table, amusing herself and her friends by repeatedly sticking a sharp knife in the table between her spread fingers. Pablo was fascinated and asked to be introduced. Her name was Dora Maar. She spoke Spanish fluently.

She was a robust woman with a round, unsmiling face. While she seemed calm and stoic, she had a fierce temper, and her moods could be as dark as Pablo's, perhaps even darker.

Although French by birth, Dora had grown up in Argentina, where she had learned to speak Spanish. She had returned to Paris to establish herself as an artist and photographer. Pablo invited her to rue la Boétie and to Boisgeloup to take pictures. Dora entered into a relationship with Pablo with her eyes open. She could not, however, anticipate the emotional storms that lay ahead.

In February, soon after he had met Dora, Pablo's friends organized a Picasso show in Barcelona. It was the largest show of his works held in Spain, and it was staged as a big event. Éluard, who gave the opening lecture, was supposed to explain Picasso's art, but he was too deeply involved in politics to make himself or Pablo understood.

Just the same, the show was well attended. It emphasized recent work, and the volume of work alone was impressive.

The critics, however, were guarded, and when Pablo's obscure poems were read over Barcelona radio, they seemed to support the claim of some critics that Pablo was nothing more than a hoax. The show had a better reception when it later moved on to Madrid.

Although Pablo did not attend the Barcelona opening, the interest in his show rekindled his urge to paint. In March, he left Paris for the south of France. He was alone and not at all sure where he would stay, but he took his paints and his sketch pads with him. He was ready at last to begin again. He eventually settled in Juan-les-Pins, sent for Marie-Thérèse and Maya, and went to work.

Pablo's output was astonishing. When he returned to Paris, he had a trunk filled with new work. He had been away less than two months, but he had explored a full range of themes and styles. There were sketches of Marie-Thérèse with a face shaped like a crescent. There was also a portrait of her painted in the style of a stained-glass window. There were minotaurs in bullrings. There were family scenes, including a bearded father watching a baby, a woman at a dressing table, a woman looking in a mirror. There were beach scenes and still lifes. And there were dark women holding each other in what seemed like mortal fear.

Pablo was not pleased with the work, but at least he had made a new start. He had Sabartés put the trunk in storage. It was not taken out again for several years. Pablo next turned to animal drawings for a natural history book that Vollard planned to publish. He also promised to illustrate Éluard's latest book of poems.

At night, he and Dora Maar visited the cafés in Montparnasse. At the same time, he visited Marie-Thérèse regularly. Although she did not suspect that Pablo had a new lover, Dora knew about Marie-Thérèse and Maya. It was a complex arrangement: Dora lived at home with her parents, who knew nothing about Pablo. When she stayed away at night, she said she was visiting friends. Pablo spent his weekends with Marie-Thérèse and Maya. On top of all this, Pablo also had Olga's nagging letters to deal with. It is remarkable that he continued to work at a furious pace.

Sabartés, who saw all Pablo's women as threats to his position, did not like Dora Maar. The feeling was mutual. Later, Dora forced Sabartés to move out of the apartment.

Pablo insulated himself from current events. He saw politics as an unwanted distraction from work. Thus, his work at this time did not reflect the approaching tragedy.

Europe was headed for another war. Fascism under Benito Mussolini's guidance in Italy and Adolf Hitler's in Germany threatened democracies everywhere. Communism, another threat to freedom, was winning support partly because of its opposition to fascism.

Most of Europe's democratic governments lacked both the energy and the conviction to make a stand against fascism, and the Fascists were eager to test their strength. The test came in Spain.

Civil war there began on July 18, 1936. Francisco Franco, the archconservative general, attacked Spain's liberal republican government. Those who backed Franco, including most landowners and the Catholic church, called themselves Nationalists. Their goal was to overthrow the republic.

At first it seemed like a minor revolt by an army general, but it very quickly turned into one of the cruelest and bloodiest civil wars of all time. And it set the stage for World War II.

Hitler and Mussolini backed Franco. The Communists sided at once with the Republicans. Democratic countries, although generally sympathetic with the Republicans, tried to remain neutral. The French government, terrified that the conflict might spread into France, did nothing to help either side. Even official statements were carefully guarded to maintain neutrality.

With his native country involved, Picasso could no longer ignore politics. Barcelona, where most of his friends lived, was united against Franco. It was unthinkable not to support his friends. Thus, Pablo became a Republican and spoke out against Franco at every opportunity.

Soon after the fighting began, the Republicans named Picasso director of Madrid's famous Prado Museum. It was a symbolic gesture, intended to win international support. An astonished Pablo accepted the appointment eagerly, but he did not know what to do. It took several weeks for him to realize the Republicans just wanted to use his name. Later, when Franco threatened Madrid, Republicans trucked the museum's treasures to safety in Switzerland. Pablo was nothing more than a bystander in this rescue. A few days later, the Prado was bombed.

There were hundreds of earlier outrages. On August 19, 1936, just a month after the fighting had begun, Franco's troops executed Federico García Lorca, Spain's most famous poet and playwright.

It took time for the full tragedy of the conflict to penetrate Pablo's indifference. During the first summer of the war, he vacationed on the French Riviera with Dora, the Éluards, the Zervoses, and other friends. He had rented rooms in a hotel at Mougins, a small town overlooking Cannes. Although the news from Spain was dire, Pablo enjoyed himself with his friends. And he worked.

He and Dora and the Éluards went to the beach or explored the back roads of the Riviera in Pablo's big, chauffeur-driven car. One day they went to Vallauris, a town founded by the Romans. It had a long tradition as a pottery-making center. Pablo watched the craftsmen turn clay into pots and then bake them in ovens. The process intrigued him.

One day, when riding in another car, Pablo was in a minor accident. He was uninjured, but the incident upset him so much that he could not work for two weeks. In September, he had himself driven back to Paris for a visit with Marie-Thérèse and Maya. He decided to move his secret family to the suburbs of Paris. He also decided, later in the year, that he needed new living and working quarters. The apartment at rue la Boétie was full of bad memories, and the studio was cluttered. He and Dora began searching for new space.

Not far from her parents' home, Dora found an old, seventeenth-century building at 7, rue des Grands-Augustins with a vacant, two-level loft. Law offices occupied the lower levels, and the loft could be reached only by a dark, spiral staircase. These features appealed to Pablo.

The two levels of the loft, also connected by stairs, could be converted, with little work, into two large studios. The top level had some small rooms that could serve as living quarters. The first day he saw it, Pablo decided to rent it. He had a bathroom installed and moved in early in 1937. Always reluctant to give up property he owned or rented, Pablo retained the apartment and studio at rue la Boétie, but he worked there rarely.

News from Spain worsened steadily. On February 8, 1937, Málaga, Picasso's birthplace, fell to Franco. Italian planes strafed refugees as they fled the city. Pablo was outraged, and he began to use his art to express his feelings.

An engraving of this period depicts Franco as a bloated bladder spewing death. *Dream and Lie of Franco* was engraved on two plates in a series of panels something like a comic strip. Showing dying horses, weeping women, and women with dead children, it was a forerunner of the antiwar statements that were to come.

On April 26, 1937, the war's tragedy came to Guernica, a town of seven thousand Basque peasants in northern Spain that had no military significance. It was late in the afternoon of a market day when German bombers screamed out of the sky. Bombs crashed. Machine guns chattered. The crowded

132

In the **Dream and Lie of Franco,** *12⅜″ × 16⁹⁄₁₆″, Pablo depicted Franco as a hairy, destructive bladder that wreaks havoc on Spain. The work was done in 1937, the same year that Pablo did his famous mural* **Guernica.**

streets turned into mayhem. More planes came, dropping incendiary bombs. Guernica went up in flames. People who were not blown up, shot, or trampled tried to escape into the fields. The planes swooped down after them with guns flashing.

The terror lasted more than three hours. When the smoke lifted, 1,654 lay dead. There were 889 wounded. Guernica was rubble.

The German military leaders were delighted with the outcome: Guernica proved that aircraft alone could destroy a town. But the free world was shocked. Never before in modern times had a civilian population been a prime target.

Pablo was stunned by Guernica. He had sided with the Republicans mainly to support his friends. It took the destruction of a small town to define the enemy and bring home the awful reality of war.

He opened his studio to refugees. Thousands were now fleeing into France. Homeless Spaniards made Picasso's studio their headquarters. Many slept there.

Meanwhile, Pablo yearned for a way to express his hatred of Franco and alert the free world to the dangers of fascism. He also wanted to vent his outrage and horror with war.

The Republicans filled Pablo's needs perfectly. They had already asked for a mural, to be used in the Spanish pavilion of the world's fair to be held in Paris in the summer. Pablo had been thinking of something decorative in Spanish theme and style, but the day after Guernica, he began working on a new set of sketches.

As his images took shape, a new style emerged. It was a kind of symbolic cubism. He used simple shapes to strongly depict his images. There were little color and no details that might divert the viewer. He drew a bull, serene, dominant, and frightening. He drew a disemboweled horse screaming at the sky. The bull and the horse came from his memory of the bullring. He drew a screaming woman, a woman with a lamp, a mother holding a dead child, a mutilated body, a body falling in flames, and a running woman.

Because it had to be a portable mural, Pablo planned the painting on a huge canvas, eleven feet, six inches high, and twenty-five feet, eight inches wide. At first, he had no idea how to bring his many images together. He solved the problem by making paper cutouts of the images and pinning them to a studio wall. It was a trick he had learned from Don José.

Pablo moved the shapes again and again. Dora Maar photographed each trial composition. At last, Pablo was satisfied. He picked up a brush and his paints and began transferring the final composition to the canvas. Pablo had never before worked on such a large surface. A stepladder was needed for the top portion of the painting. Otherwise, the scale of the work did not seem to bother him.

He used black, white, and gray, partly because these were the colors of the newspapers and magazines that published the current war pictures. In some places, Pablo laid down a texture of broken, horizontal lines that resembled columns of newspaper type.

He called it *Guernica*, but he put nothing in the work that suggested any specific time or place. He did not even sign it. He wanted the painting to be a timeless protest against war.

From the very first, viewers of *Guernica* began trying to explain the symbolism. As usual, Pablo would not comment. When asked if the menacing bull represented fascism, he shook his head and said it could be brutality and darkness. When someone said the disemboweled horse represented Spain, Pablo said that it could represent the people. But these explanations were too simple.

Symbols mean different things to different people, and Pablo wanted his painting to be the same way. The main meaning, he believed, must be the meaning that the viewer discovers. Only in this way would the painting produce the strong, personal emotion that Pablo wanted to evoke. This was another reason for limiting his palette. He knew that many different colors could defuse the emotional impact he wanted to create.

Guernica was at once controversial. Even the Republican officials who ordered the work were divided. But when the mural went on display, praise far outweighed criticism. *Guer-*

Guernica, $11'5'' \times 25'6''$, is perhaps the greatest antiwar creation in the history of art. The stark work does not rely on color for emotional impact. Instead, it simply brings together images evoked by Picasso's outrage over the brutal bombing of a Basque town.

nica proved to be a major attraction at the fair.

One viewer told an interviewer that she could not claim to understand the work, but each time she looked at it she felt she was being cut to pieces. Such statements pleased Pablo immensely. Christian Zervos devoted a whole issue of his magazine to *Guernica*. It included several articles in praise of the artist, a series of Dora Maar's photographs showing the step-by-step development of the composition, and a poem by Éluard honoring Pablo.

In conjunction with the fair, the Petit Palais, a major Paris museum, organized a show for modern artists who had been generally ignored by the French government. "Masters of Independent Art," as the show was called, filled a special room with thirty-two Picassos. The room, however, was to one side of the main exhibition hall, and at the opening reception, the room was not even shown to the president of France and other officials.

The government, it seemed, still had strong reservations about Picasso.

Exhausted by *Guernica*, Pablo and Dora, followed soon by the Éluards, returned to Mougins. There was a new passenger on the drive south. Kazbek, a recently acquired Afghan hound, loved riding in the big car with the wind in his ears. For the next several years, Kazbek would ride with Pablo everywhere he went.

Dora caused a break between Pablo and Sabartés. Jaime moved out of rue la Boétie, but in Mougins, Dora found two Spanish sisters who agreed to return to Paris and run Pablo's household. Although the younger sister soon left, the older girl, Inez, continued on the job for years. Even after she married and started a family, she remained. She was beautiful and frequently sat for Pablo. Each Christmas he presented her with a new portrait of herself.

Guernica had generated many new ideas and images. At Mougins, Pablo developed the weeping-woman image. Although most of the weepers are highly abstract, Dora Maar's features are usually easy to see.

When resettled in Paris, Pablo picked up his relationship with Marie-Thérèse. He painted several portraits of Maya, now two and a half years old. Some depict her with charming reality. Others use playful distortions.

Late in 1937, Pablo sent a plea to the American Artists' Congress, then meeting in New York, urging artists everywhere to support Republican Spain. But nothing could help. He tried to get his mother to flee to France. Doña María refused.

Soon after the new year, Franco's planes began bombing Barcelona. In a total of seventeen bomb raids, thirteen hundred Barcelonese were killed and two thousand wounded. Pablo was frantic with worry until he learned that his mother had survived.

As Republican Spain crumbled, Fascist ambitions soared everywhere. On March 11, German troops marched into Austria. The democracies did nothing. Even Pablo knew enough about politics to be able to predict the dark years ahead.

14

———— ✦ ————

WORLD WAR II

Back on the French Riviera for the summer of 1938, this time in Nice, Picasso took the opportunity to visit Henri Matisse. The old friend and rival was delighted to see Pablo.

Although they were already perhaps the two most influential artists of modern times, one could not have been more different from the other.

Matisse lived in the tidy apartment of a hotel that overlooked the sea. There was no clutter. Everything was clean and orderly. The houseplants and tropical birds that Matisse loved to paint were all carefully arranged.

That summer, Pablo was painting men and women satisfying crude gluttony with ice-cream cones or all-day suckers. These were cruel, pessimistic paintings. They showed humanity at its worst.

Matisse's work, on the other hand, had no hints of pessimism. He painted serene nudes, windows open to the warm light of the Mediterranean, sunny interiors, and decorative still lifes. While Pablo was constantly making fresh starts, always searching for another style, Matisse had long ago discovered the methods that best suited him. His main goal was to communicate his happy nature and confident outlook to the viewer.

Despite their differences, or perhaps because of them, their mutual respect had grown over the years. Pablo had purchased several Matisse paintings, and the two had also traded canvases.

Pablo enjoyed his first visit with Matisse so much that he went back to the neat apartment a few weeks later for another chat. He intended to go back that summer for a third visit, but he never did.

Guernica traveled to Scandinavia, England, and the United States. Pablo hoped it would rouse people to the Republican cause, but it was too late. Franco had taken possession of most of Spain.

In Munich, Germany, representatives of European democracies, trying vainly to preserve peace, let Hitler take Czechoslovakia without opposition. It was a shameful sellout of a defenseless ally. Pablo and most of his close friends were shocked.

When he returned to Paris, he was convinced that war was coming and that Paris would be one of Hitler's first targets. He visited Marie-Thérèse and Maya and decided they were far enough from the city to be safe from bombs.

In the fall of 1938, Pablo patched up his friendship with Sabartés and persuaded him to return to work. With Inez running the household, however, Sabartés's main duties were to admire Pablo's paintings, listen to him talk, and accompany him on his travels around the city.

Photographer Guylas Brassaï, an old friend, began taking

pictures of Pablo and his work for a photo essay commissioned by *Life* magazine. Pablo allowed pictures of himself at cafés or with friends in the studio. Pablo showed his paintings and played with Kazbek for Brassaï, but he would not allow any pictures to be taken while he was at work. The creative process, it seemed, was out of bounds. Perhaps Pablo was superstitious. He may have had the primitive fear that the camera could steal his magic.

Shortly after Brassaï shot his last picture, Pablo suffered a painful attack of sciatica. He could not leave his bed for days on end. Sabartés nursed Pablo by day. Dora Maar took the night shift. Pablo tried to work. He said drawing helped him forget the pain in his back and leg.

The fate of Spain had become a constant worry. Barcelona was crowded with a million refugees. Food was scarce. Pablo had not heard from his mother, who lived in the heart of the city, for weeks. She was now in her eighties.

Barcelona fell on January 26, 1939. Refugees flooded into France. Many came to Paris and sought help from Pablo. By then, the sciatic pain had eased and he was able to walk, but he soon heard the news he feared. Doña María had died in Barcelona on January 13. Although she had died of natural causes, Pablo would always speak of her as one of Franco's victims.

The fall of Barcelona brought the terrible war to an end.

Pablo decided at last to move his residence from rue la Boétie to the studio. The latter, however, was often so crowded with Spanish refugees that he had to retreat to the apartment or else move in temporarily with Marie-Thérèse and Maya. This left Sabartés to deal with the refugees while Pablo worked.

He painted dismembered, disjointed women, weeping in despair or screaming in terror. One painting showed a cat eating a bird. His anguish over Spain and his fear for France seemed to show in everything he did.

Pablo's international popularity reached new heights in 1939. New York alone had six Picasso shows, including the Museum of Modern Art's "Picasso, Forty Years of His Art." There were other shows in Chicago, Los Angeles, London, and Paris.

Summer brought escape from bustling Paris. Pablo went south again, this time to Antibes. He wanted to do a major work there but was diverted by sad news.

Ambroise Vollard, the dealer who had been selling Pablo's work as long as anyone, died in Paris on July 22 after suffering a head injury in an auto accident. Pablo hurried back to Paris for the funeral. When he returned to the Riviera, he brought Sabartés with him.

Dora Maar did not object, and the poet, who needed a vacation more than anyone, was delighted with the warmth and soft light of southern France. Pablo and Jaime took long drives together, leaving Dora at home. The two went to a bullfight in the chauffeur-driven car.

The defeat of Spain and the death of his mother had strained Pablo's emotions. His relationship with Dora had cooled. Pablo needed his old companion desperately. At one low point, Pablo told Sabartés that his work was everything. Without it, he would kill himself.

Pablo had set up a large canvas in the apartment, but for several weeks he could not decide what to do with it. His inspiration came one night when he and Dora took a stroll along the Antibes waterfront. Girls were passing them on bicycles. In the harbor, fishermen with spears had rigged lights to their boat to attract fish. Pablo and Dora walked home in the moonlight, eating ice-cream cones.

The evening left Pablo with a strange, dreamlike impression filled with exciting images, which he painted onto the big canvas. His *Night Fishing at Antibes* is a highly abstract composition with several light sources, including the stars, the moon, and the fishermen's lights. It shows the boats, the

Picasso also had the Spanish civil war much in mind in 1939 when he painted **Night Fishing at Antibes,** *6'9" × 11'4". The indifference of the girls to the cruelty of the fisherman parallels the world's indifference to the Spanish tragedy.*

COLLECTION, THE MUSEUM OF MODERN ART, NY MRS. SIMON GUGGENHEIM FUND

harbor seawall, a man spearing a fish, the bicycles, and the girls, one of which is Dora eating ice cream. The mood of the night is set with serene purples, blues, and greens. Against this, Pablo showed the cruelty of the spearman and the indifference of the girls, reflecting, perhaps, the world's indifference to the fate of Spain.

On August 23, Germany and Russia surprised the world by signing a nonaggression pact. It was now clear that Hitler wanted a stable eastern front in order to give full attention to war in the west. News of the Russian pact caused some panic in France. Pablo did not know whether to stay on the Riviera or go to Paris. After two days, he had the car loaded with all the food and extra gasoline it could carry and sent it off to Paris. There was room for the driver, the rolled-up *Night Fishing at Antibes,* and Kazbek. Pablo, Dora, and Sabartés took the train.

He did not know what to do about all his paintings. Those in shows throughout the world were safe, but the bulk of his work, including many statues, was scattered and unsorted in his Paris studios. He decided to pack everything and find a safe place to store his treasures outside the city, but when he faced the job, it was too big.

Where should he begin? He paced and lit cigarettes, filling both lofts at the studio with smoke. Friends in the French government warned Pablo that war would be declared in a matter of days. He needed a haven.

Pablo picked Royan, a little north of Bordeaux on the Atlantic coast, for his retreat. It was far from Paris, and Marie-Thérèse and Maya happened to be vacationing there. The big car was crowded when he left Paris on August 29. With him were Dora, Sabartés, and Mercedes, Sabartés's friend, Marcel, the chauffeur, and Kazbek, the dog.

On their arrival in Royan, Pablo learned that permits were required for all refugees. He returned at once to Paris, had the permits signed, and was back in Royan on August 31.

The next day Germany invaded Poland, and the war began.

Nothing happened in France. There was tense anticipation everywhere, but no guns could be heard. Paris was not bombed. The only change in Royan was that the crowds were refugees, not tourists. Dora and Pablo took rooms in a hotel. Dora had no idea that Marie-Thérèse and Maya were living in a nearby villa. And Marie-Thérèse still did not know of Dora's existence.

Carrying on a double life in a small resort town diverted Pablo from worrying about his various Paris studios and the art he had done nothing to save. His story to Dora was that he had rented a studio in the villa and had to go there to work. His story for Marie-Thérèse was that his work at the hotel kept him from visiting her as much as he wished. He played this game successfully for several weeks.

At various times during his stay in Royan, he made quick trips to Paris in the big car. On one trip, he saw herds of horses headed for slaughter. Pablo drew them as the first sacrifices of the war. Later he drew sheep skulls, often giving them large jaws and threatening teeth. These gave way to distorted human faces, often cruel and menacing.

He had no easel, but by propping his canvas on a chair back, he was able to work with his usual diligence. He changed styles frequently. His *Still Life with Sheep,* painted on October 6, was harshly realistic. His *Woman in an Armchair,* done two weeks later, used such grotesque distortions that it looked like a vision from a dream.

Sabartés worked on his biography of Picasso. The project was the main topic when he and Pablo strolled about town and visited cafés. The book, called *Picasso: Portraits and Souvenirs,* was not published until after the war. It contains much bias in Pablo's favor. Sabartés was too fond of the artist to even hint at unfavorable facts.

When the government demanded the villa at Boisgeloup as barracks for French soldiers, Pablo took another trip to

Paris to make arrangements. Unfortunately, the ignorant soldiers were to destroy much of the sculpture Pablo had stored there. These proved to be his worst war losses.

Back in Royan, the inevitable happened. Marie-Thérèse saw Dora Maar getting out of Pablo's car. He said Dora was a Spanish refugee seeking his help, but Marie-Thérèse was not fooled or amused. Pablo tried to act as if nothing had happened, but he could not ignore the tension. Eventually, he rented another apartment where he could escape from both women, but he still visited each daily.

Although Poland was quickly divided by Germany and Russia, the final months of 1939 brought a long lull that became known as "the phony war." The Allies used the time to try to prepare their defenses. But it was not long enough.

Pablo spent his time painting and drawing. He filled several sketchbooks with bullfight scenes, studies of hands and heads, and many drawings of women. Early in March 1940, he painted *Woman Dressing Her Hair.* It depicts a repulsive female tending to her hair with a horrid kind of pleasure. Despite extreme distortion of limbs and facial features, the painting is a realistic and intimate summation of human vanity.

Soon after finishing this strange painting, he made another visit to Paris. This time, he took Dora with him and stayed in the city several weeks. Many friends were in the army, but most had frequent furloughs and were able to drop in on Pablo. He and Éluard discussed the poet's next book, which Pablo had promised to illustrate. Zervos had scheduled a show of Pablo's watercolors. This had to be discussed. Pablo, reluctant to return to Royan, prolonged his stay. Paris seemed to be safe.

On May 10, however, with shocking speed, the Germans invaded Belgium and Holland. Three days later, after outflanking the French army, the Germans headed for Paris. On May 16, Pablo and Dora made a fast retreat to Royan.

All coastal communities were now flooded with refugees. Some of Pablo's friends planned to sail from Bordeaux to safety in the United States. They tried to persuade Pablo to come with them. He refused. What would happen to his paintings if he left France?

There was an unsettling sense of urgency and fear in Royan. Pablo stayed in his hotel and worked.

On June 3, while Hitler's armies were sweeping into France, Pablo began filling a new sketchbook with drawings. He drew several pictures of Kazbek, and he did a view of Royan from his window, which would be repeated in a painting a few months later.

The Germans occupied Royan on June 23. Some German air force officers set up headquarters in the hotel next door to Pablo's. He kept working.

So far there had been no gunfire. After a few weeks, Pablo began to gain confidence. Peaceful survival under German occupation was beginning to seem possible.

On August 15, however, a sentry at the German headquarters next door was killed by a bullet, and that evening a shot was fired into the apartment below Pablo's. Although the French police managed to convince the furious Germans that the shots could have come from an airplane, Pablo's worries were revived. He was an alien in an occupied country, and he had done nothing about getting the documents that the Nazis required of aliens. Furthermore, he was an artist, a modern artist.

The Nazis, looking on most modern art as degenerate, had already destroyed numerous modern masterpieces. Many German artists had either fled the country or given up painting. How would the Nazis deal with Pablo?

Fortunately, the German position on art was being modified. Hitler wanted to appear more liberal than he actually was. He hoped to win the French over as allies, and he wanted to negotiate peace with England. Although there was no formal policy on art, it soon became clear that the Nazis were not going to persecute an artist as famous as Picasso.

Pablo decided to move back to Paris. There, he could get his alien papers signed and be close to his paintings and his sculptures. And, of course, it would be easier to work in his own studio.

The Nazis had set up a puppet government in France. The Vichy government, as it was called, employed several of Pablo's friends. Some of these friends gained influential positions in the regime. This situation added to Pablo's sense of security. Indeed, his friends in the government would soon help him through some serious difficulties.

He lived at first at rue la Boétie, but he soon decided to move into the studio, partly because it was close to his favorite cafés. Dora Maar had done the renovations necessary to make the living space comfortable, but the lofts were hard to heat. This would be a problem all through the occupation because of the shortage of coal.

Although coal was rationed, Nazi officials frequently offered Pablo extra fuel and food with the hope of bringing him into the Nazi camp. A few words of support from Picasso would have been valuable propaganda for Germany. Although he refused the bribes, Pablo was able, through connections in the Vichy government, to get extra rations of fuel each month. Unfortunately, he used up his coal long before the month was over. This caused many days and nights of stoic suffering.

A few lesser-known artists did side with the Nazis. These collaborators, as they were called, publicly and privately attacked Picasso and his art. The most troublesome collaborator was Maurice de Vlaminck, who had long regarded Pablo as an archrival. The occupation gave Vlaminck an opportunity to attack Pablo and his work. Vlaminck wrote that Picasso had dragged French painting into a dead end.

He also accused Pablo of lacking creativity and borrowing all his ideas from other painters.

Pablo could not answer the attacks without attracting unwanted attention. Some of his friends wrote cautious rebuttals, but newspapers and magazines during the German occupation could print only the most moderate defenses of modern art.

He was later accused of being a Jew and of having underground connections. The gestapo, or Nazi secret police, were obliged to look into such an accusation. This caused Pablo much trouble and worry. The fact was that he did have underground connections. Éluard had joined the underground and would sometimes hide at Pablo's studio and even hold meetings there with other members of the underground. It was a risky game.

Like many who survived the occupation, Pablo had friends in both camps, the Vichy government and the underground. Under the circumstances, it was wise to have many friends.

When the gestapo came to rue des Grands-Augustins to check Pablo's papers, search for anti-Nazi propaganda, or look for other evidence of underground activity, Pablo usually had advance warning.

One invaluable friend throughout the occupation was André-Louis Dubois, who had once been assistant head of the French national police. Although he had not been able to keep this post under the Vichy regime, Dubois had many connections in government. It was Dubois who saw to it that Pablo's alien registration card was quietly renewed, and it was usually Dubois who warned Pablo when the Germans were coming to inspect his studio.

Most Germans knew nothing about modern art, and this, on at least one occasion, was fortunate for Pablo. When the Germans decided to inventory all bank vaults in order to tax valuables, Pablo had to take Nazi inspectors to the two vaults he rented in a bank basement. The vaults held his collection of Cézannes, Renoirs, Rousseaus, Matisses, and other valuable paintings, along with some of his own work. Luckily, Pablo took the art dealer Pierre Colle with him. The Germans could not understand why such a collection of "inept" paintings was in a vault. Pablo's face turned red with anger. He might have told the inspectors the true value of the work, but Colle kept him silent and answered the Germans' questions with enough shrugs and mumbles to save Pablo from paying a heavy tax.

Pablo rarely went to cafés or galleries. He did not try to exhibit his work. He accepted no invitations. He worked hard and stayed as inconspicuous as it was possible for a famous artist to be.

From time to time during the occupation, German artists who appreciated Pablo's work called on him. Pablo greeted them cordially and showed them around his studio. To do otherwise would have attracted attention. Besides, with fellow artists Pablo could overlook political differences. Pablo enjoyed giving the Germans postcard reproductions of *Guernica* as souvenirs of their visits.

Some Paris art galleries had been taken over by agents for German collectors. Pablo unwittingly sold paintings to these dealers, but he stopped as soon as he learned they were serving the Nazis.

The Nazis' conservative views on art were imposed on the art schools of Paris. Teachers were encouraged to condemn modern "degenerates." Teachers who did not support this position were soon replaced. A generation of art students thus emerged from the war with little taste for, or understanding of, modern art.

Jean Cocteau at first won friends among the Germans by endorsing Arno Breker, a sculptor who did massive statues of athletic males that pleased Hitler. Pablo, for a time, regarded Cocteau as a collaborator and refused to see him. By 1943, however, when it had become clear that the Germans would eventually lose the war, Cocteau withdrew his support of Breker and other official artists. He and Pablo became friends again.

Kahnweiler had fled Paris when the Germans arrived and had gone into hiding in the south of France. His sister-in-law, Louise Leiris, continued to keep the gallery running. Throughout the war, Louise and her husband, Michel, were among Pablo's closest friends.

But Pablo's friendship with Max Jacob was strained. Although Max had converted to Catholicism, the Nazis discovered his Jewish heritage and forced him to wear a yellow star, the identification required of all Jews. It was not healthy to be seen often with a Jew. Before the war ended, Jacob was put in a Nazi detention camp, fell ill, and died.

The arrest of Nazi resisters occurred frequently. Executions were common. Often the victims were well known to Pablo. Some had been visitors at rue des Grands-Augustins.

Meanwhile, women continued to be an important part of his life. Marie-Thérèse and Maya returned from Royan in the winter of 1942. Pablo found an apartment for them, which he visited every Thursday and Sunday, the days Maya was home from school. Pablo also continued to see Dora Maar regularly, and occasionally he called on Olga and Paulo, who was now twenty-one years old.

Women again dominated his painted images. He gave them grotesque features. Some had crossed eyes and hornlike noses. Many were weeping. Some wore flowered hats, the kind that Dora liked to wear. In 1943, however, these images gave way to figures with more pleasant, youthful features. Pablo had found a new woman.

15

LIBERATION

Because he rarely went out, Picasso's artistic production during the occupation reached new peaks. Despite hardships and distractions, he scarcely missed a full day of work.

Women's heads, seated women, nudes, portraits, bullfight scenes, monsters, and even some cubist works were typical of the period. He did two sensitive portraits of Nush Éluard. He continued to paint portraits of Dora and of Inez, the housekeeper. He also turned out several animal etchings to illustrate a natural history book. And he returned to sculpture.

The bathroom at the studio was the only room with adequate heat. Pablo turned it into a sculpting studio. He spent hours there, modeling with clay or putting together found objects. He made a *Bull's Head* by mounting bicycle handle-bars on top of a bicycle seat. The sculpture was simple, humorous, and powerful.

Pablo sculpted a large head of Dora in clay, which he wanted to cast in bronze for the much-discussed monument for Apollinaire. He also did *Flayed Head,* a stark skull that skillfully combined rough and smooth surfaces with deep excavations for mouth, nose, and eyes.

There were several recurrent themes in his paintings. A favorite theme depicted two women, usually one asleep and the other at the foot of the bed, watching. Sometimes the watching woman had a musical instrument. In one picture, one woman is washing the other's feet. In another, one women is lifting a curtain to reveal the other asleep. Two women and a child provided a variation. In one charming picture, a woman is helping a child takes its first steps.

Among Pablo's many sketches was the repeated image of a man holding a sheep. This led to a large statue that Pablo completed in a single day in 1943.

The sculptor Julio González died after a long illness on March 27, 1942. Pablo somehow linked the loss with the Spanish tragedy and did a series of seven paintings, each showing a bull's skull against a green and purple background. González, who had worked for many years with Pablo at Boisgeloup, had never achieved fame. He had been overshadowed by Pablo. Pablo liked to dramatize this by telling friends that he had "killed" González.

He might have said the same of Dora Maar. She developed a serious mental disorder during the war. The long illness and then death of her mother upset her, and Pablo infuriated her by his regular visits to Marie-Thérèse and irregular visits with other women. Dora, never a cheerful person, suffered spells of deep depression. She attempted suicide. Pablo was not sympathetic. Sometimes she would lie in a kind of coma, oblivious to Pablo's insults. Other times she would suffer violent fits brought on by nervous tension. The fits frightened Pablo. But even though Dora clearly needed professional care, Pablo did not get help for her. His many portraits of her usually show her weeping.

He made little effort now to keep Marie-Thérèse and Dora apart. One afternoon, Dora found Marie-Thérèse at rue des Grands-Augustins and ordered her to leave. Pablo put his arm around Marie-Thérèse and said she was the only woman he loved. This gave Marie-Thérèse the courage to tell Dora to leave. She refused. As an amused Pablo watched, the two women began slapping each other.

Eventually they left separately.

Although he rarely went out, Pablo did enjoy a few hours from time to time at Le Catalan's, a café in the neighborhood where he could meet friends and have a good meal. Even there, he drew, covering napkins and tablecloths with sketches. Sometimes he painted on the tablecloth with wine, coffee, gravy, or mustard. He also made paper cutouts. His friends were delighted, and Pablo was pleased with the attention.

Life in Paris became more difficult and more dangerous in 1943. Rationing of electricity began early in the year. Thirty metro stations were closed to conserve power. On February 8, five students, suspected of organizing an anti-German demonstration, were shot by the Nazis. The gestapo began to intensify its search for Jews. Pablo had been friends with the Rosenbergs, Kahnweiler, Max Jacob, Gertrude Stein, and many other Jews. The Germans took this as proof that Pablo himself was Jewish.

One day, two gestapo agents came to rue des Grands-Augustins. Pablo had to let them in and take their insults. They called him a degenerate, a Communist, and Jew, but they did not arrest him. They simply left, promising to return again. They never did.

Once, some high-ranking German officers, who had come to see and admire Picasso's art, came face to face with Paul Éluard, who was wanted for his activities with the Communist underground. Fortunately, he was not recognized.

Éluard and his wife, Nush, were hiding in a mental hospital where a friendly doctor had certified them as patients. But Éluard, a friend since cubist days, was a frequent visitor at the studio and spent hours trying to persuade Pablo to join the Communist party.

One evening in May of 1943, while dining with Dora and some friends at a favorite café, Pablo noticed two young girls at a nearby table. He attracted their attention with loud talk. Later he offered them a bowl of cherries. He learned that the girls were painters and invited them to visit his studio. Dora Maar watched this flirtation, knowing from experience that she could not stop it.

The next day, when the girls called on Pablo, he made it clear that he was particularly attracted to one of them. He asked her to come back again. She did.

Françoise Gilot was pretty, had a quick mind, and was dedicated to art. She was twenty-one. Pablo was sixty-one. She would be the important influence on his life and his art for the next seven years. She would bear two of his children.

The transition from Dora to Françoise was gradual. As expected, Sabartés was cool to Françoise. Inez, however, was friendly and did her best to ease Françoise into Pablo's life while easing Dora out. Françoise herself had misgivings about starting a relationship with a man almost three times her age. Her parents certainly would not approve. She waited almost a year before becoming Pablo's mistress, and two years passed before she began living with him.

Pablo, however, began drawing and painting his new woman at once, and, as soon as her youthful, oval face appeared in his work, Dora Maar knew she had serious competition.

The Allies landed in Normandy on June 6, 1944. Pablo's first fear was that Paris would be destroyed. He decided to leave the city and take all his paintings with him to some safe refuge. But again the job was too big. Besides, where could he go?

After a few days, news came of the Nazis' slow retreat before the massive invasion force. Pablo decided to stay in Paris and keep working. Work helped him forget his fears. He painted several street scenes at this time. Apparently, he wanted to preserve the views he loved before they were destroyed. He also painted several versions of a tomato plant that grew in his studio and had finally begun to bear fruit.

As the Allies approached, the city became sharply divided. Nazi collaborators urged reprisals against the underground and those who were sympathetic with it. Pablo believed his enemies had once again turned him in to the gestapo. But the gestapo did not come to the studio and it was alive with activity.

While members of the underground planned street campaigns to help the invading Allies, other friends talked of fleeing the city or at least finding safe places to hide. Dora Maar left Paris.

When it seemed certain that street fighting would start, Pablo moved into Marie-Thérèse's apartment. He hid there throughout the battle of Paris. The Germans did not resist for long, although newspapers made much of the battle. It was even suggested that Pablo had taken an active role in it, but he had spent the time painting.

He did women's heads and a portrait of Maya. He also did a watercolor based on *Triumph of Pan*, by Nicolas Poussin, an influential French artist of the seventeenth century. Poussin had depicted a wild picnic of men and beasts in a full range of emotions. The picture delighted Pablo, and his version kept him occupied until the end of August when the Allies gained control of Paris.

Pablo returned to the studio as a hero.

The American press created the image. Although his work had not been shown in France during the war, it had been exhibited often in the United States, and at least seven new Picasso books had been published since the war had started. When the shooting stopped in Paris, the world had to know at once if Pablo Picasso had survived.

The simple fact that he was alive and healthy turned him into a symbol of liberation. His survival was equated with the survival of art and freedom. Everyone wanted to meet him and shake his hand. Ernest Hemingway, one of the first correspondents in Paris, had called at the studio while Pablo was still at Marie-Thérèse's. The famous novelist had left a box of hand grenades. What better gift could a "freedom fighter" wish?

Correspondents who called a few days later found Pablo at home and demanded interviews. Pablo did nothing to discourage the heroic image. After all, he had survived and he had continued to produce art. *Life* photographer Robert Capa took pictures of the artist with *Man with the Sheep* and other recent works. Capa's pictures gave proof to the world that the creative spirit will never die.

In no time, the studio became almost as important to tourists as the Eiffel Tower. With Inez or Françoise serving as interpreters, Pablo gave tours to hundreds of American soldiers. He signed autographs and let his picture be taken with his visitors.

Cocteau warned Pablo against encouraging attention. The poet feared that reporters might discover that Pablo had welcomed German visitors to his studio and even sold some paintings to Nazi dealers. Éluard angrily responded to Cocteau by saying that Pablo was one of the few artists who had behaved properly during the occupation.

Éluard by now had great influence in the Communist party, and the Communists, because of their work in the resistance, enjoyed respect in the days that followed liberation. *Les Lettres Françaises,* a Communist journal, praised Pablo's conduct during the occupation.

On October 5, 1944, Pablo joined the Communist party.

Perhaps Pablo's decision was inevitable. He was an idealist. He equated communism with peace, justice, and equal opportunity. Joining was much like a religious commitment for Pablo. He said it was an act of faith.

Pablo had always been treated as an alien in France. He would not return to Spain. He told one friend that becoming a Communist was like coming home. Éluard, at the moment, had Pablo's greatest respect, and Éluard, as everyone knew, desperately wanted Pablo to join.

Several friends argued against the step, but they had little influence. Pablo might have listened to Kahnweiler, who opposed political involvement, but the dealer had not yet returned to Paris. Gertrude Stein, at the time, had no influence at all.

She and Alice Toklas had spent the occupation in the French countryside. Even though she was a Jew, Gertrude was not persecuted during the war because of Bernard Faÿ's protection. Faÿ, a translator of one of her books and a good friend, had held a high position in the Vichy government. Thanks to him, Gertrude's Paris apartment had been sealed to prevent the Germans from confiscating her art treasures as Jewish property.

After the war, Faÿ was sent to prison, along with other high-ranking collaborators, while Gertrude and Alice enjoyed almost as much popularity among the American soldiers as did Pablo. Like Pablo, their primary achievement had been survival, and survival was worth honoring.

On October 7, a large show of Pablo's work opened in Paris's Salon d'Automne. Seventy-four paintings and five sculptures gave a fair sample of his diverse and imaginative work during the occupation. The work ranged from the *Bull's Head* fashioned from a bicycle seat and handlebars to large paintings of distorted faces and figures.

The show, opening two days after Pablo became a Communist, was intended as a tribute. It was received with violent demonstrations and loud protests. Students ran through the gallery demanding that the work be removed. Some paintings were temporarily removed for safekeeping.

Many of the demonstrators represented the conservative attitudes taught by Germans during the occupation, but some protests were prompted by the French middle-class resistance to modern art, which had existed long before the war. The middle class was also strongly anti-Communist.

The opening demonstrations were followed in a few days by a second outburst. This time, students were able to remove a few paintings, but they were quickly recovered, undamaged.

The demonstrations, of course, attracted much attention and assured the show's success. Many young artists, Françoise Gilot included, volunteered to stand guard beside the paintings. The press generally sided with Pablo. And French intellectuals demanded artistic freedom for Comrade Picasso.

Despite the support, Pablo was upset, particularly because so many young people, whom he saw as the artists of the future, did not respect his work. And after all the favorable publicity he had received, he was shocked to discover that some people did not like him, his art, or his politics.

Meanwhile, prices for his paintings took a sharp drop. During the war, the United States had been the strongest market. When he joined the Communist party, prices in the U.S. plunged.

When Kahnweiler returned to Paris, he persuaded Pablo to make a public explanation of his political commitment.

His statement, printed by the Communist press in October, concluded:

"I have always been an exile, now I no longer am; until the day when Spain can welcome me back, the French Communist party opened its arms to me, and I have found in it those that I most value, the greatest scientists, the greatest poets, all those beautiful faces of Parisian insurgents that I saw during the August days; I am once more among my brothers."

Most perceptive readers could now see that Pablo was sincere and a little naive. After a few years, Pablo's political zeal cooled. He learned that the Communists, much like the Nazis, had some very restrictive ideas about what art should be.

Artistic freedom was a luxury most Communists could not support. The conservative faction of the party attacked Picasso's work as unintelligible. Shouldn't art be understood by the masses? Pablo, as usual, did not try to explain or justify his work.

Meanwhile, his postwar fame made him even more attractive to young women. Sabartés tried to discourage what he called "the young hot pants." Some simply wanted autographs or his name on a political petition, but most were eager to share his bed. Pablo usually obliged. When Sabartés became troublesome, Pablo simply made appointments to meet his admirers at rue la Boétie.

At the time, few people knew of this "schoolgirl" phase of Pablo's career. Certainly Françoise Gilot, who had still not moved in with Pablo, had no suspicions. She had been taken to Bateau-Lavoir, where Pablo recounted his invention of cubism. She also had been taken to Gertrude Stein's, where she won the approval of both Gertrude and Alice Toklas, not an easy achievement.

Dora Maar, instead of making a break with Pablo, kept herself available, but the calls for a lunch date with Pablo or a quick visit to his studio became rarer and rarer. Her mental health did not improve.

Finally, after police found her one night wandering in a confused state near the Seine, Pablo put her under a doctor's care. Dora was no longer the proud woman who had fascinated Pablo in a Paris café in 1936.

Although Pablo's Communist party membership had depressed prices for his works, they had not slowed sales. Kahnweiler, once again the major Picasso dealer, did a brisk business. Pablo also let Louis Carré offer some paintings in his fashionable gallery, and he occasionally dealt directly with American dealers.

In business, Pablo could be rude and abusive. Kahnweiler, his most loyal dealer, could shrug off the abuse, but most of the Americans did not know how to handle Picasso. One American arrived at the studio with high expectations and lots of cash, but it was the man's new London hat that Pablo admired. He said if the man brought him a hat just like it, they might do some business. The dealer rushed back to London and returned the next day with the hat. Pablo accepted it, but he never let the dealer have any paintings.

Pablo's work during the occupation had little to do with the war. After the liberation, however, he turned to war themes. *The Charnel House* and *To the Spanish Republicans Who Died for France* were large pieces reminiscent of *Guernica*. They were not, however, as successful. The still lifes he painted in this period with cooking pots, skulls, and candlesticks received more acclaim.

On his first postwar vacation, Pablo took Dora to Cap d'Antibes. Françoise, still undecided about her future, went to Brittany. Before long, however, she received a letter from Pablo, urging her to join him. She refused, but as the summer progressed she realized that it was hopeless to resist Pablo. On November 26, 1945, her twenty-third birthday, she moved into the Paris studio at rue des Grands-Augustins.

16

✧

LIFE WITH FRANÇOISE

A few days before Françoise made her decision, Pablo's interest in printmaking revived. This time, however, instead of making etchings and engravings, he wanted to do lithographs.

Drawing on a limestone slab with a crayon was faster and more direct that etching or gouging metal plates. He had made a few lithographs prior to the war, but then etching had been his chief interest. In the fall of 1945, however, Georges Braque urged Pablo to visit Fernand Mourlot's shop on the rue de Chabrol.

It was a famous shop, where theatrical posters dating back to the late 1800s were once mass-produced to announce performances of Sarah Bernhardt and other stars. Mourlot had inherited the shop from his father, who had purchased it in 1914. On November 2, 1945, when Pablo paid his first visit, Mourlot employed the world's best and most inventive lithographers.

Watching skilled craftsmen at work was both an inspiration and challenge to Pablo. Perhaps Braque knew this, but no one, least of all Pablo, suspected that he would return to Mourlot's daily for the next four months.

The workers were at first skeptical of the artist's interest. Other artists had come to the shop with ambitious plans for prints, but they never had the patience to master the technical problems of lithography. Pablo, however, decided to do a serious body of work. The very fact that he began arriving at the shop at 9 A.M., long before his usual hour of waking, was indication enough of his dedication. He ordered Sabartés to tell no one what he was doing. While at Mourlot's, Pablo would tolerate no interruptions.

Mourlot assigned Pablo to a corner of the shop where an old and experienced worker, Tutin, had charge of one of the presses. On his first day, Pablo made a quick drawing of a woman's head directly on one of the stones. Soon he was eyeing the proof that Tutin pulled from the press.

He quickly settled into a routine. After Marcel the chauffeur dropped him off each morning, Pablo would stroll briefly about the neighborhood before joining the workers. He would chat with them for a few minutes and then retreat to his corner.

Mourlot and his workers very quickly recognized Pablo's skill, dedication, and energy as unusual assets, and Pablo soon appreciated the potentials and the limitations of lithography. He set out to explore the potentials and challenge the limitations.

Tutin, the shop veteran, was not enthusiastic about Pablo's art, and besides, Pablo wanted to do things that Tutin thought impossible. Mourlot, however, had been wise in selecting Tutin as Pablo's helper. The old printer was proud and stubborn. He always found a way to get the results that Pablo wanted.

Tutin's obvious dislike of Pablo's images prompted the artist to make some wild creations. Often Pablo would ignore advice and still get excellent results. The other workers were fascinated. No one could predict what would come from Pablo's corner.

He did several women's heads, giving most of them Françoise's features. He also did heads of boys, still lifes, nudes, and bullfight scenes. Later he began making prints for poet Pierre Reverdy's *Hymn for the Dead.* The early lithographs were black and white, but after a few weeks he started making color prints.

Pablo saw accidents as part of the creative process. He would not let his printers strengthen a weak line or correct any other defect on the stone. Because saliva, even small drops, makes whites spots on a lithographic image, printers traditionally mask their mouths when working over a stone. Pablo refused to wear a mask. The white spots, he declared, were part of the process.

His bold use of the stone fascinated the workers. He loved to put one image or idea through several changes. After pulling a set of proofs from a stone, he would change the image, pull more proofs, and then change the image again to create a whole series of prints that gave variations on a single theme.

Pablo's bull series became the talk of the shop. The first proof showed an ordinary but somewhat fat bull. After inspecting the first proof, Pablo used an erasing solution on the stone to thin the bull down. The second print, or second state, as printers call it, showed a slightly thinner animal. It was still not what Pablo wanted.

He erased some more and pulled the proof on a third

state—still not right. He put the stone aside for several days, but he did not forget it. Eventually a fourth state, then a fifth appeared. Pablo attacked the stone with a scraping tool to erase unwanted portions of his image.

Finally, after six weeks, Pablo was satisfied with the eleventh state of his bull. It was almost a stick figure of the animal, but it was unmistakably a Picasso bull.

Completing the series seemed for a time to satisfy Pablo's hunger for lithography. He would work in Mourlot's often again, but he would not stay more than a week or two at a time.

Life with Françoise was not what Pablo had imagined. She had a very complex personality. Most of the young girls in his life so far had been interested only in Pablo the man. Françoise was interested in Pablo the artist.

A good artist in her own right, she was not afraid to speak her mind about Pablo's work. Although her praise was genuine, she was too sincere to flatter Pablo. His ego received some serious jolts.

Pablo's criticism of other artists caused some heated arguments. It was a surprise to her that Pablo felt threatened by some of his contemporaries. It seemed the great man lacked confidence.

She had her own confidence crisis. Her middle-class family could not accept the bohemian life-style. As long as she was Pablo's mistress, she remained on bad terms with her family, particularly her father. She was troubled by guilt, which often caused long periods of silence. Pablo never fully understood Françoise. The girl fascinated and puzzled him.

During the first few months of their relationship, Pablo painted Françoise again and again. When at Mourlot's, he drew her face from memory. In the studio, he had her sit for portraits. His most famous Françoise painting, *The Flower Woman*, was painted early in May of 1946. Pablo had grown dissatisfied with the realistic portraits he had done of his new mistress. They were too passive, and Françoise definitely was not the passive type.

One day, using pastel shades that he handled so well, he began to simplify her form, reducing her image in much the same way as he had reduced his bull through various states at Mourlot's. Soon his canvas showed little more than a long, thin body topped by a round face. He had turned Françoise into a plant in bloom. But it was not yet a portrait. He put his brushes aside and made oval cutouts of various shapes and sizes from light blue paper. A few lines on each oval turned it into Françoise's face. Next, he pinned the ovals to the canvas, one by one, to test his composition. He moved them, stepped back to look, and moved them again. This continued until he finally placed an oval he liked in a position that pleased him.

The final step was simple. He marked the position of the paper with charcoal and then carefully painted the oval in light blue. When he added the simple lines of the face, the painting was finished.

One of Pablo's more abstract portraits, *The Flower Woman* looks like a sculpture with a wire body and ceramic plates for breasts and face. A series of loops around the face can be seen as flower petals or as hair. The pastel tones suit Pablo's view of Françoise's character perfectly.

A month after the picture was painted, however, Françoise was threatening to leave him. Pablo was angry with her, but he would not give her up. He declared that he could not go on living without her. Françoise agreed to stay.

There were many other fights and reconciliations. In the spring of 1946, she threatened to leave again. She even wrote to her mother to say that she was coming home. A few days later, however, she and Pablo began planning their summer vacation in the south of France.

Françoise thought they would stay at Saint-Tropez,

Cannes, or one of the other famous beach resorts. She could hardly believe it when Pablo announced that they would stay in Dora Maar's house in Ménerbes, a provincial village far from the coast. Pablo had given the house to Dora several years earlier. She had rarely used it.

The house was somber. The villagers were not impressed with Picasso and not pleased to have him living in their town with a young mistress. There were just the three of them—Françoise, Pablo, and Marcel. Françoise soon began to look upon the chauffeur as a guard. The summer itself, she saw as a test. Pablo talked often about Dora and he read the frequent letters from Marie-Thérèse aloud.

Finally, she could take no more. She left the house one morning and tried to hitchhike to Marseilles. Her plan, once there, was to get on a boat for North Africa.

The first car to stop for her, however, was Pablo's. He had Marcel drive them back to Dora's house. Instead of ranting at her, Pablo described their future together in glowing terms. He told her she needed to have a child.

Françoise was not convinced. She might have tried to flee again if Marie Cuttoli, the famous weaver who had once turned some of Pablo's designs into tapestry, had not come for a visit. She urged Pablo and Françoise to visit her summer place at Cap d'Antibes. By now, even Pablo had had his fill of Ménerbes.

One look at the beach from Marie Cuttoli's house was all he needed. He sent Marcel back for their luggage at Ménerbes and rented two floors of a house in nearby Golfe-Juan.

The beach, with its young bathers and brilliant sun, inspired a return to mythology for Pablo. He drew centaurs, nymphs, and fauns. He sometimes colored these drawings. The work reflected his happiness.

They had arrived on the Riviera just in time for the annual potters' fair in nearby Vallauris, the old Roman town he and Dora had visited with the Éluards before the war. This time,

Françoise and Pablo met Georges and Suzanne Ramié, who were trying to reestablish their Madoura ceramics shop, one of the oldest in town. The Ramiés, who hoped Pablo might design some pottery for them, suggested that he mold something from some balls of clay that were sitting on a workbench. Pablo quickly fashioned two bulls and a faun and promised to return to see them in a few days after they were fired.

He had asked many questions about the shop and the pottery craft, but that summer he did not return to see his little creations as promised. The Ramiés, keenly disappointed, assumed that Pablo had shown interest only to be polite. But this was not the case. As usual, seeing craftsmen at work had inspired him. He promised himself to work with clay, but he knew it would take a full summer to test the medium.

Meanwhile, he fell into another project. One day on the beach at Golfe-Juan, Pablo was introduced to Ramuald Dor de la Souchère, curator of Antibes's new art museum. The museum, in a large château, was almost empty at the time. Dor de la Souchère hoped Pablo would provide some work.

Pablo agreed at once to donate some drawings, but later during the conversation, Pablo said that he longed to paint on a large scale. Dor de la Souchère immediately invited Pablo to take a look at the bare walls of his museum. It was just a few steps away.

Above the ground floor, the bare white walls seemed to beg for decoration. Pablo wandered about. He said nothing, but his imagination ran wild. In his mind's eye, the walls of the château came alive with fauns and centaurs. He told Dor de la Souchère he would begin work at once.

Pablo set up a studio on the third floor of the château and installed the wiring and lights he needed to paint day and night. He next stocked the studio with gallons of boat paint and dozens of broad brushes. Soon, the mythological figures he had begun drawing as soon as he arrived at Golfe-Juan began to dance across the walls. He also drew many figures in his classical style. All were happy images, but he stuck to muted colors and simple compositions.

There were many walls to cover. Although he usually worked all day and far into the night, the project kept him at Golfe-Juan until December. In his spare time, he carved figures of birds, bulls, and fauns on pebbles that he and Françoise had found on the beach.

The long stay in Golfe-Juan worried the Communists. Had the party's most famous new member abandoned Paris for a life of luxury? Éluard assured party officials that Pablo was simply on a honeymoon. Rumors of the work in the Antibes museum, however, touched off new concerns. Fauns, centaurs, and other mythological figures did not conform to the party's policies on art. What did these murals have to do with the social problems of postwar Europe?

Pablo's murals drew criticism from the general public as well. When the museum was finally opened, there were protests and even some attempts at vandalism. Pablo, however, had come to expect controversy. If he tried to please everyone, his work would mean nothing to anyone.

Picasso's reputation in America received a big boost in 1946, when the doors opened in New York on the Museum of Modern Art's "Picasso: Fifty Years of His Art." It displayed works from every phase of Pablo's long career.

There were scores of other Picasso shows in Europe and America. Books about him blossomed in the postwar surge of publishing. He seemed to be overcoming the art world's anti-Communist elements. Just the same, Pablo felt out of touch with current developments in art.

Public tastes had changed. Nonobjective art, scorned before the war, was becoming popular. Despite Pablo's abstractions and wild distortions, he never totally abandoned the recognizable object. In fact, he disdained nonobjective work, but now he seemed to be alone.

Matisse, who had been an important touchstone for Pablo, was an invalid. Gertrude Stein, who seemed indestructible, had died while Pablo and Françoise were at Golfe-Juan.

Braque was still painting, but at the moment, Pablo was avoiding his old friend. This was due largely to the critic Jean Paulhan, who wrote repeatedly in books and articles that Braque had been the primary inspiration for cubism. Although Braque was not responsible for Paulhan's views, it took Pablo a long time to get over his resentment. Meanwhile, Pablo claimed that he himself had invented cubism, and he spoke bitterly of Braque.

Françoise was not on good terms with Éluard, who blamed her for Dora Maar's mental illness. Pablo, however, welcomed and encouraged visits from both Éluard and his wife, Nush. On November 28, 1946, however, Nush died unexpectedly in Paris. Pablo himself was badly shaken by the news. Éluard was almost out of his mind with grief.

Pablo returned to Paris late in the year, expecting to renew his artistic contacts. He was disappointed. Few painters of his generation could be found, and it seemed that all the young artists were now living and working in New York. Gradually, Pablo began to realize that the prewar Paris he loved could not be revived.

Perhaps it was time for a change. Pablo could expect a change in his personal life. He learned that he, at age sixty-six, was going to be a father. He bragged about this news to everyone, but Françoise was not thrilled.

And Jaime Sabartés was unhappy. A baby would further diminish the poet's authority in the household. Sabartés, who relished Pablo's company, realized he would enjoy even less of it. Inez also was not thrilled. She and her husband, living in the same building at rue des Grands-Augustins, had earlier had a baby who had received much affection from Pablo. Although Pablo painted another portrait of Inez and her child, she knew that her baby would have a rival.

Pablo, however, seemed to be insensitive to any resentment. He strutted proudly about the studio and in and out of his favorite restaurants.

One day he took Françoise to the vaults where he kept his collection of art. The bank guard, an old friend, remarked that most visitors appeared year after year with the same women, but Pablo never seemed to come with the same woman twice. The observation pleased Pablo immensely.

He took Françoise and Paulo to Boisgeloup. The silent villa might have depressed him, had it not still been filled with his large sculptures. He was not tempted to reactivate the studio, but had no intention of giving it up.

Pablo said he was too excited about becoming a father again to undertake any major projects. But he did some oils of his centaurs, fauns, and other mythological figures, and he also did some illustrations. His visits to Mourlot's were sporadic, but just the same, he completed fifty lithographs.

One lithography venture in the spring of 1947 opened a new source of inspiration. Pablo had always taken ideas, styles, and even color schemes from other artists and changed them into creations that were distinctly his own. So far, this had been largely an unconscious effort. Now he decided to take the works of old masters and very deliberately develop his own variations. It was something like taking an old folk song and orchestrating it into a modern piece of music, except in Pablo's case, the results would have little resemblance to the original.

His first source of inspiration for this method was the sixteenth-century German painter Lucas Cranach. Cranach's *David and Bathsheba* seemed to Pablo to be a happy combination of ritual and eroticism. The lithographs based on the painting show nothing of Cranach's style and no more

171

than a hint of the original composition, but the prints capture the spirit of Cranach's painting exactly. Pablo worked on his Cranach series off and on for two years.

Drawing inspiration from the old masters appealed to Pablo's sense of tradition. It was a way of paying tribute to artists he admired. Although Don José might not have liked the results, he would have approved of his son's respect for the past.

On May 15, 1947, Françoise gave birth to a son whom they called Claude. A delighted Pablo pointed out his own features on the boy's tiny face and told his friends that it was not possible to mistake the relationship. Pablo was bursting with pride when he took his new family to Golfe-Juan for the traditional summer vacation. Maya, now eleven, accompanied them.

17

---><---

FAREWELL TO PARIS

Françoise could not escape from Pablo's past lovers. Maya reminded Françoise of Marie-Thérèse. Paulo, who appeared at Golfe-Juan with his wife and children, reminded her of Olga, and Olga herself wrote daily letters that Pablo read with much comment.

Françoise seemed more sensitive to family problems than did Pablo. After Paulo separated from his wife, he was a frequent visitor at Golfe-Juan. His idleness bothered Françoise and Pablo tried to find some job that would interest his son, but nothing satisfied Paulo.

It was Olga, however, who caused Françoise the most concern. Pablo had given up all thoughts of divorce, and as long as he remained married to Olga, Françoise could never become Pablo's wife. As if this were not enough, Olga came to the Riviera and began following Pablo and Françoise around.

It was bizarre. When Pablo and Françoise went walking, Olga would appear behind them, telling all the onlookers who may have gathered that she was Mrs. Picasso and the girl with Pablo was merely his mistress. When Françoise went out alone, Olga taunted her with shouts and curses.

Pablo asked the police to keep a sharp eye on his wife. This subdued Olga for a time, but then she accosted Pablo and Françoise on the beach one day. The meeting ended in a hair-pulling battle between the two women. There was no clear victor, but the contest, much to Pablo's chagrin, drew a large audience.

Pablo by now was accustomed to fame. Most of the attention delighted him, but the scandal sheets could be unmerciful. These tabloid newspapers and cheap magazines loved to print photos of Pablo with various women. People with cameras began stalking him as if he were a wild beast. Pablo tried to ignore it. Françoise hated it.

Pablo said famous people had to expect such things.

He had not done much work since Claude's arrival. Before leaving Paris, he had designed the sets for a production of *Oedipus Rex,* but there were too many distractions for steady work in his studio.

When he arrived at Golfe-Juan, Dor de la Souchère called at once to remind him that the work at the museum was not yet finished. The project no longer held Pablo's full interest. He wanted to sun himself on the beach with Françoise and the new baby.

Françoise Gilot in a pensive mood became the subject for one of Picasso's many prints during his postwar campaign in the lithograph shop. This lithograph, 24½" × 18½", was printed in November 1950.
COLLECTION, THE MUSEUM OF MODERN ART, NY

One day, while on the beach, he and Françoise again met the Ramiés. They reminded him that he had left some small figures at their pottery shop in Vallauris the previous summer. Why didn't he come and see them? Suzanne Ramié recalled later that she never expected Pablo to accept the invitation. Pablo, however, was hungry for a new challenge.

That very day, Marcel delivered Pablo and Françoise to the Ramiés' factory. Pablo brought several sketches with him. He explained to the Ramiés that the sketches were ideas for pottery projects that he had thought of during the previous winter. If he could have some technical help from a workman, he would try to turn the ideas into reality.

The Ramiés were delighted. They had been struggling to win back their prewar markets. Having Picasso's name associated with their shop would bring undreamed-of attention, not to mention profits.

It took a few more days to finish his work for Dor de la Souchère. Then he was ready. Pablo was eager to roll up his sleeves and join the craftsmen. In a way, he was repeating the experience he had enjoyed at Mourlot's lithography shop. Again, he amazed the workers with his quick grasp of the technical skills. His intensity, daring, and unfailing judgment soon became the talk of the shop.

Three-dimensional work, of course, was not new to him. He had made sculptures with clay, as well as with metal and wood. Now, however, he wanted to make three-dimensional objects that would be both functional and pleasing to the eye. He drew on tradition for his designs, following forms he remembered from his studies of Greek and Mycenaean pottery. The amphorae used to store olive oil, grain, wine, and other cargoes of ancient times provided a favorite pattern. Although he gave his pieces the general shape of amphorae, Pablo always added something that was distinctly his own.

At their potter's wheels, the shop craftsmen turned pots to the size and general dimension that Pablo wanted. Then

176

he would mold designs or add pieces to the wet clay. Sometimes, while a pot was still turning, he would use his thumbs to form it into a woman's torso. Then he might add arms for handles to complete the piece.

He did things with the clay that none of the workmen had ever attempted. As usual, when Pablo became the center of attention, he became even more daring and more creative than ever before. The workmen gathered around to hear him discuss each piece. He was candid with them, freely admitting his mistakes or pointing out something he might have done to improve a pot.

After a day's work in the pottery, Pablo was always willing to treat the workers to drinks. He could be excellent company among so many admirers. Meanwhile, Pablo's presence in the shop established the workers as elite members of their trade. Even the Communists approved of Pablo's pottery phase, not because of his creations, but because he was associating with workers.

In order to be closer to the workshop, Pablo rented a small house at Vallauris. Later, to provide room for his family, he bought Villa la Galloise, the biggest house in Vallauris. Françoise was delighted with the move because it provided an escape from Olga, who had become a permanent resident of Golfe-Juan.

Pablo's enthusiasm remained at a high pitch. He rarely missed a full afternoon of work in the Ramiés' shop. Sometimes he turned out as many as twenty-five pieces in a single session. The summer heat, combined with the heat of the kilns, could be almost unbearable, but that did not keep Pablo from working. He stuck to this schedule for more than a year, turning out almost two thousand pieces of pottery.

That summer, Jean Cassou, newly appointed curator of the modern art museum in Paris, called to say that the government at last wanted to buy some Picassos. Pablo was so pleased he offered to give the French museum some work.

When the curator arrived to pick them up, he was surprised and delighted to be presented with twelve paintings.

Pablo was very proud. Until that moment in all the official government collections, there had been just one Picasso, a portrait painted in 1901, which had been stored in the government collection among the work of foreigners. Now Pablo would be well represented. Included in his donation were *Nude with a Musician, The Milliner's Workshop, Enamel Cooking Pot,* and *Still Life with Oranges.* Later, in memory of his wife, Éluard gave the museum the portrait of Nush that Pablo had painted in 1941.

Unfortunately, Pablo's generosity did not prompt the French government to add to the collection with further purchases of any substance. The government was even reluctant to put up $100,000 to help Dor de la Souchère complete the work needed to open the museum in the Antibes château.

Although Pablo did little painting during 1947, he found time, when not in the pottery shop, to work on etchings and engravings. It was his interest in pottery, however, that kept him in the south through the winter and into the summer of 1948.

There were a few quick trips to Paris, but he avoided any major interruptions until late August of 1948. Although he hated travel, Pablo, at the urging of Éluard and other Communist officials, agreed to attend the Congress of Intellectuals for Peace at Wroclaw, Poland. Marcel drove him to Paris, where the two of them, joined by Éluard and other Communist officials, would fly to Poland. Before going to the airport, however, the French government, now run by the Socialists, awarded Pablo the Silver Medal of French Gratitude for services rendered to France. Although this was a political rather than an artistic award, Pablo was extremely proud of the honor.

Scores of famous writers and artists from around the world attended the peace conference, but Pablo drew the most

178

attention. At countless meetings and ceremonies, he was hailed as a brother, a friend, and the greatest artist of his age. He gave a speech defending the Communist poet Pablo Neruda, who was then being held in jail in Chile. Pablo was given tours of Warsaw and Cracow as well as Wroclaw. In Cracow, an art museum closed since World War II was reopened in his honor. The president of Poland gave him an award for his work in improving relationships between France and Poland, another political honor.

Pablo, basking in the attention, wanted to see everything. Thanks to earphones and a team of interpreters, he was able to follow every session of the conference. He was keenly interested in world peace and was delighted with his role as a participant. Domestic peace was another matter.

Although he had promised to write to Françoise often from Poland, he never did. Instead, he had Marcel send daily telegrams, a deception Françoise saw through, because Marcel always closed with *bons baisers,* a working-class salutation that Pablo would never have used.

Françoise was certain by now that Pablo was having affairs with other women. When he returned to Vallauris, she gave him an icy greeting. It did not seem to bother him. As soon as possible, he returned to the pottery shop and settled into his routine.

The first exhibit of his pottery was held in Maison de la Pensée Française in Paris during November of 1948. The show brought a new round of critical acclaim.

Pablo went to Paris for his shows, to see dealers, and to inspect his studios, but the city now had little to offer him. The nonobjective art that he had never learned to like dominated the galleries and museums. Most young artists regarded him as a historical figure, not part of current art movements. He enjoyed working a few days at Mourlot's and he liked to call on Kahnweiler and other old friends, but he was soon eager to head south again. By 1948, he had decided to live there permanently. This, of course, did not mean that he would give up any of his Paris studios.

Pablo continued to play games with dealers. When the American dealer Samuel Kootz came to Paris soon after the war with a suitcase bulging with money, Pablo used Kootz's offers to raise the prices he got from Kahnweiler. Kootz agreed to meet any price, but Pablo always made him wait several months before closing any deals. He wanted time to be sure Kahnweiler learned of the competing offers.

Once, Pablo let Kootz have a painting in exchange for an American car, a white convertible that the dealer had shipped to France. Pablo continued to sell paintings to Kootz until an alarmed Kahnweiler finally obtained exclusive purchasing rights on all future Picassos. Even after this, however, Kootz was always a welcome visitor at Pablo's home. He used the American to keep Kahnweiler on edge.

After Pablo left Paris, Fernand Mourlot went south at least once a month to bring fresh lithography plates and pick up the ones Pablo had finished. Thus, the illustrations were finished on more portable zinc plates rather than stone. Pablo continued to do illustrations, but he focused on etchings and engravings rather than lithographs.

It was a lithograph, however, that captured the greatest public attention in the postwar era. He had done it at Mourlot's on January 9, 1949. It was a white pigeon against a black background. In preparing the stone, Pablo had diluted a wash to produce the light, delicate tones in the feathers and shadows. It was an image he had worked on before. Pigeons, in fact, dated back to his childhood when he had watched his father paint the birds.

Pablo knew them as cruel birds that bullied and sometimes killed weaker members of the flock. It was thus ironic that the pigeon should be picked as a peace symbol. The Communist official who came to Pablo in search of a poster to announce the next peace conference knew nothing about pigeons. To him, Pablo's bird looked like a dove, the dove of peace.

Pablo let the official take the print for the poster. There was no time to lose. The conference, to be held in Paris, was scheduled for April. The poster was designed quickly and printed by the thousands. Within days, Pablo's "dove" was circling the world. It appeared everywhere—in galleries, libraries, museums, workshops, student dormitories. Even in America, where the Communist peace campaign was regarded with suspicion, the poster won acceptance. The Philadelphia Academy of Fine Arts gave it an award. In the years to come, Pablo would do other peace posters showing real doves, but none would match the fame of the poster for the 1949 peace conference.

Back at Vallauris, Pablo went regularly to the Ramiés' shop, but he did not work with the same intensity as before. He had begun painting again. His favorite model early in 1949 was his son, Claude, but he also painted several portraits of Françoise. In addition to the painting, he continued to work on etchings and lithographs.

Françoise was pregnant again. Neither she nor Pablo was very happy about it. The two had been arguing repeatedly. Françoise was humiliated and angry over Pablo's infidelities. She had been thinking of leaving him. For her, the pregnancy was another complication in a life that was already complicated enough. Pablo's feelings showed in his portraits. He dissected her on the canvas. He turned her face into an inhuman mask. Sometime red and brown forms oozed from the mask. For Pablo, Françoise had become a vision from a bad dream.

The baby, a girl, was born on April 19, 1949. They named her Paloma, Spanish for dove. She was Pablo's last child.

Paloma's arrival calmed the household. For a time, the arguments were forgotten. For a time, Pablo kept his other women in the background.

Françoise wanted Villa la Galloise to be clean and simple. The only decorations were some paintings and a few ceramic plates. This did not reflect Pablo's love of clutter. He needed more space of his own.

He rented an abandoned perfume factory, a large L-shaped building hidden behind a forest of weeds. For a time, Pablo pastured two donkeys to control weeds in the front yard. They fertilized the ground so well that the yard became a garden of wild mint and daisies.

The inside of the studio was not so tidy. Pablo filled the building with found objects, tools, statues, canvases, paints, brushes, and several things that defied definition. Dust and cobwebs soon mantled neglected corners. One arm of the L was for sculpture. The other was for painting and etching. There were small side rooms for storage. Each large room had a big potbellied stove.

Arriving at his studio late in the morning, Pablo would poke about a bit and stoke the stove, if necessary. Then he would set to work. If he had friends with him, he would suggest, sometimes not too politely, that they leave. Most friends left quietly.

On days when Pablo wanted company, he would go to the beach, spend a few hours with family and friends, and then depart alone for his studio or the Ramiés' shop.

He began making large statues with found objects. *Centaur* and *Animal Head* were among the earlier pieces. Later he did the life-size *Pregnant Woman,* with a round washbasin for the swollen stomach. *She-Goat,* the most famous piece from this period, was later cast in bronze.

Pablo and Françoise Gilot revel in the climate of the French Riviera, a region that would soon become their permanent home. Fin Vilato, a friend, laughs at the high jinks.

PHOTOGRAPH BY ROBERT CAPA, MAGNUM PHOTOS

In the summer of 1949, he shifted his energy back to painting, doing innumerable portraits of Claude, Paloma, and Françoise. He also drew inspiration from old masters. He did *Portrait of a Painter, After El Greco* and *Young Ladies along the Seine, After Courbet.* In each picture, he tried to express the mood of the original, without giving up anything of his own style.

In June of 1950, after North Korea invaded South Korea, the United States sent troops and arms to South Korea. The Communist party, in a large propaganda campaign, attacked the United States as an aggressor nation. Pablo was expected to provide something to be used in the Communist campaign, but he had little interest in events on the other side of the world. Even though his Communist friends deplored America's role, Pablo remained detached.

He had already donated art and posters to the party. He had signed petitions and given money. He had not, however, given freely or promptly. People had to plead before he would do a painting or a drawing.

No one begged him to do something about the Korean bloodshed, and Pablo, by now, had become a little unhappy with the party's views on art. His art did not comply with the "social realism" that the Communists wanted.

The Communist position on the abstract and nonobjective art dominating Western Europe and America in the postwar years was that it was decadent. This echoed the stand the Nazis had taken on art they could not understand.

No official rules on art could possibly influence Pablo. He had always painted for himself. Éluard and other Communist friends respected his position, but many others, including some party leaders, were both puzzled and upset. If a man is a Communist, they reasoned, he should paint like a Communist.

Pablo had joined the party, in large part, to escape isolation. He expected the party to support his work. He could not see how his art could cause any problems.

Early in 1951, he began working on a large canvas showing armed warriors attacking naked victims. Like *Guernica*, it had little color. It was mostly metallic gray, with touches of green and yellow. Pablo finally called it *Massacre in Korea*. Although it showed human suffering, it did not have the impact of *Guernica*. Unlike Spain, Korea was remote to Pablo both in geography and in spirit.

The painting was exhibited at the Salon de Mai in the spring of 1951. It drew no raves. Even the leading Communist reviewer had a mixed reaction, calling it "important" in one sentence and "modest" in another.

On top of this, Pablo soon learned that the party's central committee had ordered all Communist publications to mention *Massacre* as little as possible. The boycott left Pablo dumbfounded. When the painting came back to Vallauris, he set it up outside his studio and stared at it for a long time, trying to understand what could possibly be objectionable about it.

At this point in his life, it seemed that the town of Vallauris, with its simple people, was far more friendly than his chosen political party. The villagers greeted him daily. They were obviously proud of their famous resident. Pablo appreciated their smiles and their laughter.

He had already given the town one of several castings of his *Man with the Sheep*, a life-size statue he had made in 1943. He thought it was one of his best sculptures. The statue had been standing in the town square for a year when he offered to do a mural in a nearby abandoned chapel. The town leaders accepted the offer at once, but before Pablo could start work, the building had to be repaired. By the spring of 1952, however, all was ready.

Pablo had wanted to build a "temple of peace" on a

mountaintop on the Spanish border, but the project, though much discussed, never materialized. It was still a possibility, however, when he began working in the old chapel. Ideas for a mural were thus already going through his head when he began the preliminary sketches for the chapel. He decided to make it his temple of peace.

He filled two sketchbooks. They helped him work out the details, but the overall plan was elusive. The small chapel had a low, arched ceiling that made it look and feel something like a tunnel.

One side of the chapel, he decided, should depict war; the other, peace. On the ceiling, he would place the sun. For the central symbol of war, he chose a horse. It pulled a hearse over books and other symbols of civilization, while menacing warriors watched from the background. For peace, he used a warrior holding the scales of justice in one hand and the shield of peace in the other. He also depicted nude women dancing, a family with a mother nursing her child, a man writing, children playing, and a boy blowing on a pipe.

While working on his temple of peace, Pablo's home life was far from peaceful. Although Françoise had been diverted from her troubles in the spring of 1952 when Kahnweiler staged a show of her paintings, she wondered, on her return from Paris, if her patience with Pablo could last another year.

Their home was both hotel and restaurant to a parade of visitors. Françoise never knew who Pablo might invite to spend the night. Sometimes, she might be surprised by several dinner guests. Other times, Pablo might vanish, leaving her to make excuses. At a railroad depot the trains came and went on time. At Villa la Galloise, there was no fixed schedule.

But worst of all, Françoise felt neglected and a little envious. The people, after all, came to Vallauris to see Pablo Picasso, not Françoise Gilot.

18

THE HECTIC LIFE

Pablo did little to discourage the visitors. He enjoyed having an audience. Even when old friends sometimes brought strangers to the villa, Pablo, if he was in the right mood, greeted them warmly. If he wanted to work, however, he retreated to the old perfume factory, where he might remain all night.

Françoise awkwardly tried to explain his absence.

Cocteau, Kahnweiler, and the Leirises were frequent visitors. Éluard came until he fell ill. Once Charlie Chaplin arrived with a friend. There was also a parade of Communist officials, art collectors, reporters, photographers, and even wide-eyed people with pens and writing pads, who wanted nothing more than Picasso's autograph.

If feeling generous, he might take a houseful of guests out to dinner. When feeling playful, he might greet his guests while wearing a mask or a costume. For a time, he liked to paint tattoos on his visitors. Friends, knowing Pablo's love of disguises, often brought him masks and costumes, but just as often Pablo made his own getups. Sometimes he made disguises for Claude and Paloma and would have them join in the fun. Françoise, however, was a spectator, not a participant.

Marie-Thérèse and Maya tested Françoise's good nature with their frequent visits. Pablo made no effort to keep the two women apart.

One day, Georges Braque and his wife received an enthusiastic welcome. At the time, Pablo was working on *Woman with Baby Carriage,* made with a real baby carriage and many found objects. Braque greatly admired the statue. Then the two friends sat down to recall old times. They had good memories of their vacation together in 1912, when the two inventors of cubism spent the summer making collages. Pablo had been with Eva that summer.

During the bullfight season, life at the villa became even more hectic. French bullfights were held in many towns in the south of France where Spanish influence was strong. Pablo and Paulo would spend hours organizing parties for a bullfight day. Marcel had been fired for smashing the car on an unauthorized outing, and Paulo had taken over as the family chauffeur. He now took a major role in the bullfight debates. When should they leave? How many tickets should they order? Who should be in the party? The discussion could go on for hours.

Pablo rarely missed a fight. His arrival in a town was greeted with blasts of car horns, shouts, cheers, and trumpets. Sometimes a band played as he stepped from his big car. He received almost as much attention in the stands as did the bulls and the toreadors in the arena.

Back home, Paulo and Pablo would review the day's

events endlessly. Françoise sometimes found it amusing, but mostly it was simply tedious.

Somehow, in all this activity, Pablo found time to write a play. Perhaps *Four Little Girls* diverted him from the domestic crisis that he must have known was coming. The play, full of puns and word associations, was praised by most of his friends, but it was not destined for glory.

On November 18, 1952, Paul Éluard, who had been sick for a long time, died. Pablo attended the funeral, which was held on a cold day in Paris. He had lost one of his closest and most loyal friends, a friend who had been an important buffer between Pablo and the reactionary elements of the Communist party.

The death of the old poet left a big gap in Pablo's circle of admirers. Fortunately, the Pignons were available and did their best to fill the gap. Édouard Pignon was a painter. His wife, Hélène Parmelin, a writer, had already started to keep a record of Picasso's conversations.

Pablo had urged the couple to settle in Vallauris, and he had provided a studio for Pignon. Pablo trusted Pignon's artistic judgment, and it was Pignon who usually had the first look at the latest Picasso canvases and prints. Pablo's close friendship with the couple continued for the rest of his life.

Meanwhile, it had become clear to Françoise that Claude and Paloma, whom Pablo loved to play with and have pose for him, were all that held their stormy relationship together. There seemed to be nothing else.

Pablo would not give up his practice of disappearing overnight or perhaps for a day and two nights to be with another woman. When he was alive, Éluard, always on the alert for young and eager nymphs for Pablo, often had arranged the trysts. But even after Éluard died, the nights away from home were as frequent as ever.

Pablo and the woman of the moment would check into a

hotel in one of the nearby resort towns. He was not discreet. He was sometimes spotted by Françoise's friends. At times, he even signed his own name on the hotel registry. This was all it took to bring the photographers. Within a few days, the tabloid newspapers would have front-page pictures of Pablo and a strange women coming out of a hotel.

Françoise had too much pride to tolerate Pablo's behavior much longer. Their raging arguments only made the situation worse. She decided to try a new tactic.

Meanwhile, Pablo had more troubles with the Communist party. Joseph Stalin died on March 5, 1953, and Pablo was asked to do a cover portrait of the Russian leader for *Les Lettres Françaises,* the major Communist journal in France.

Although Stalin had been a cruel despot, at the time of his death no Communist regarded the leader as anything other than a saint. No artist could make a portrait flattering enough to suit the party. Pablo, however, showed Stalin not as a silver-haired saint, but as an aggressive young man, hungry for power. It was not a flattering portrait, but it was published just the same. A wail of protest echoed around the Communist world. *Les Lettres Françaises* was flooded with letters of complaint. The Communist central committee officially disapproved of the portrait.

The man who had asked Pablo to do the portrait made a public apology. Newsmen invaded Vallauris to get Pablo's reaction. American reporters repeatedly asked if Pablo would now leave the party. He turned all reporters away, saying that the matter was between him and the party and would not be discussed publicly. But he was confused.

Already deeply hurt, Pablo was shocked when Françoise sided with his critics. She told Pablo the portrait had been a serious mistake. When Pablo's friends tried to modify her stand, she declared that Picasso was outdated and that the painters of her generation would lead the way. The sooner people realized this, the better.

Pablo was stunned. Françoise had never before taken sides against him. And there was something else even more upsetting. Françoise had begun to ignore his affairs with other women. When he returned to Villa la Galloise after two or three days' absence, she no longer asked where he had been. Nor did she ask about faces of strange women that appeared in his paintings and prints. Her new tactic troubled Pablo deeply. Was she indifferent? It hardly seemed possible.

He found refuge in his work. He painted still lifes, scenes of his village, heads of his women, and Paloma at play. Visits to the Ramiés' pottery shop were rare. He was putting most of his remarkable energy into paintings and prints.

During a brief stay in Paris early in 1953, he spotted a discarded zinc plate at Mourlot's. It had been used to print a poster portraying an Italian woman. The texture that had been etched in the zinc for the halftone print fascinated Pablo. He saw the plate as a found object that he could convert to something of his own.

That night, he worked on the plate at the studio, and when he brought it back to Mourlot's the next day, the image had changed. Except for dark outlines to accent some features, the image was not greatly altered. The background, however, was alive with fauns. Some danced, others made faces or played pipes. On one side, a naked woman watched with a bemused expression. Pablo's cavorting figures seemed bent on distracting the Italian woman from her calm pose. It was one of his most inventive and charming prints.

Pablo rarely attended his exhibits, even when they were near home. In 1953, there were major shows in Lyons, France, and two in Italy, one in Milan, the other in Rome. Cocteau gave the opening speech for the show in Rome, but even that did not tempt Pablo. He stayed home and was content to look at photos of the gallery rooms, when they arrived in the mail. He also received newspaper clippings with the reviews of his shows, but these he rarely read.

In the summer of 1953, Picasso was the subject of a short film that included scenes of him putting the finishing touches on the murals, entitled *War and Peace,* in the Vallauris chapel. When work on the film, also called *War and Peace,* ended, Pablo went on vacation. He took Maya with him to visit friends in Perpignan, the last major French town on the coast road before reaching the Spanish border. The place appealed to him tremendously. His hosts' house had plenty of work space. The town was close to his beloved Spain. And the mountaintop where he still hoped to build his temple of peace was not far away.

The people of Perpignan were delighted to have the famous artist in town. They encouraged his idea for the temple. Some suggested that Pablo move into a nearby castle and become a permanent resident. Pablo was interested.

This, in fact, was the first of several visits to Perpignan. Eventually, his hosts hoped that Pablo would find a place of his own in town. It was easy to entertain Pablo and his daughter, but the train of Picasso admirers was another matter.

When he returned to Vallauris, Pablo received the shock of his life. Françoise was leaving him.

What had gone wrong? Always it was he, Pablo, who decided when relationships began and ended. The women had to accept his wishes. It had never been the other way around.

And what about the children? No mother could possibly abandon her children. The children, Françoise announced, were leaving with her. Pablo was speechless.

He was desolate. Despite his behavior, his family feelings were strong. He loved his children. They had restored his youth. With them gone, he felt all of his seventy-two years.

Friends tried to console him, but for a time Pablo found release from sorrow only in his work. He designed the set he had promised for a play by García Lorca. He also did several sketches on the theme of the artist and his model. These harked back to the studio interiors that had provided the images for many of the prints in the *Vollard Suite*. It was now a familiar motif. Pablo did 180 drawings of the artist at work, with the model never very far away. All of his energy went into the drawings. Sometimes he did as many as twenty in one day.

Although Françoise's departure did not disrupt Pablo's routine or trysts with other women, many of his old friends feared that he might be lonely on New Year's Eve. Thus, a large crowd of revelers gathered at Vallauris to help him welcome 1954. The party did help restore Pablo's confidence, and he soon began painting again. An English tourist, blonde and young, agreed to pose for him. He did several portraits of her. He also painted Claude and Paloma from memory.

Pablo visited Henri Matisse several times. Although bedridden, Matisse was making bold cutouts from a variety of colored papers. Under his direction, an assistant pinned shapes to the walls, which created marvelous patterns that were later turned into the colored lithographs and paintings that are counted today among Matisse's best work.

Impressed by Matisse's creations and his spirit, Pablo was, at the same time, depressed over the man's illness. It seemed to Pablo that all his friends were either dead or dying.

Pablo himself was in excellent health. He could still work far into the night without loss of enthusiasm or energy. Despite the many reminders of death around him, he had nearly twenty more active and productive years ahead. And a new love was about to enter his life.

Jacqueline Roque, a niece of the Ramiés, had often been at the shop while Pablo was working. Pablo had met her there and had seen her often on the beach. She was a brunette with sharp features and a high-bridged nose that fascinated him. Divorced and living nearby with her

193

four-year-old daughter, Catharine, Jacqueline did nothing to hide her interest in Pablo. She had, in fact, already visited him at Villa la Galloise from time to time, when Françoise had been away on trips.

On June 3, 1954, Pablo painted his first portrait of Jacqueline. He used hard angles and strong diagonals to show her seated with her arms clasped around her bent knees. He gave her an enigmatic, sphinxlike expression.

It was at this time, in Paris, that poet and critic Louis Aragon made a telling comment on Pablo's work. In a preface for an important Picasso show, Aragon wrote that Pablo "is harder to talk about than anyone else." The point was that, whatever one concludes, there is always something in Picasso's work that contradicts the conclusion. The artist was too versatile to be defined.

The observation pleased Pablo. Hadn't he always avoided defining his work with words?

The show itself delighted the critics and the general public, because it compared early work done from 1900 to 1914 with later work done from 1950 to 1954. It included paintings from the Gertrude Stein collection and from the Soviets. The majority of the critics preferred the earlier Picassos, but some marveled at the changes and variety of styles that the master displayed.

Unfortunately, the show ran into legal problems. Soviet works had been confiscated from a private collector after the Russian Revolution. Irene Keller-Shchukine, daughter of the collector, claimed that she, and not the Russian government, owned the Picassos. She filed an injunction against the show in a Paris court. The court denied a hearing for her claim, but the show was closed and the Soviets, not wanting to risk further trouble, withdrew their paintings.

Pablo was in a delicate position. He thought that the Keller-Shchukine claim was reasonable, but he could not make any public statement without embarrassing Russia and his political party. He quietly supplied enough substitute paintings from his own collection for the show to reopen.

In August 1954, he and Maya went to Perpignan again. It turned into an eventful vacation.

Jacqueline appeared unexpectedly, and Pablo, in a surprising display of Spanish propriety, refused to let Jacqueline stay in the house with him. He insisted that she stay in a hotel instead.

This ruffled Jacqueline's normally even temper, but Pablo shrugged off her protests. He was in his element. There were lazy days on the beach and an endless crowd of admirers. The Spanish flavor and the tourist atmosphere of the town allowed Pablo to recruit followers wherever he went. Local artists paid homage. Guitarists performed for him. Cameras clicked like castanets. Crowds followed him into restaurants. When he went to the town square to watch the dancers who performed there in the warm summer evenings, the crowd was immense.

Pablo became very serious about moving from Vallauris to Perpignan. He rented two workrooms in a villa and even tried to buy a large, ugly château. It was not for sale.

When the Pignons, Ramiés, and other Vallauris friends heard that Pablo might move to Perpignan, they wrote to Jacqueline, urging her to prevent it. Jacqueline worried more about Pablo's roving eye than his future residence.

One day, when three pretty girls asked for his autograph, he told them to get their hair fixed, put on good dresses, and join him that evening at a local restaurant. The girls found themselves that night in a royal train of some twenty Picasso devotees.

Françoise, with Claude and Paloma, arrived for a visit. They stayed with Pablo and his hosts, the Lazermes, while Jacqueline remained at her hotel. It was too much. Despite Pablo's protests, she moved in with the crowd. At one point, Pablo's hosts were feeding fifteen guests. That was too much

195

even for Pablo. He asked the Lazermes to shield him from family and friends so he could do some work.

His Perpignan friends, of course, wanted Pablo to become a permanent resident. Just when it seemed he had made the decision, however, he and Jacqueline had an argument that was heard throughout the house. She left the next morning, but at midday she telephoned. Pablo refused to talk to her. She called again. This time Pablo spoke to her.

Pablo told her their relationship was over. Jacqueline threatened suicide. Pablo said good-bye and hung up. The affair, it seemed, was over. Jacqueline, however, was intelligent, shrewd, and very determined.

Two days after her suicide threat, she returned to Perpignan and once again moved into the house. Pablo was furious at first, but he soon accepted her presence. Jacqueline charmed her hosts with her excellent manners and good nature. She flattered Pablo with her attention. She called him "her God." She kissed his face and his hands in public. Pablo was not capable of resisting such attention. He gave in completely.

One friend who observed the conquest said that Jacqueline Roque was the first woman in Pablo's life who managed to lead him by the nose. Of course, Jacqueline soon led Pablo back to Vallauris.

Pablo's friends now fell into two camps—those who liked Jacqueline and those who did not. Naturally, she surrounded herself with those who supported her. As time passed, Pablo noticed that many of his old friends were rare visitors at Vallauris. But he did not protest. He let Jacqueline take complete charge of the household. She stopped the endless parade of surprise visitors, and it seemed that Pablo appreciated more order and stability in his life. It made it easier for him to work.

His many portraits of Jacqueline reveal a deep love and respect. He did not distort her face or show her weeping as

196

he did when painting his other women. Jacqueline is always portrayed with calm dignity.

Early in their relationship, perhaps to avoid certain old friends, Jacqueline chose to stay in Paris for several months. They lived at rue des Grands-Augustins, where Paris friends were welcomed, particularly on Saturdays. Meanwhile, Pablo took Jacqueline to his favorite restaurants and galleries. In Montmartre he showed her Bateau-Lavoir. They went to Mourlot's print shop and Kahnweiler's gallery. Then, a phone call brought the news that Henri Matisse, age eighty-four, had died on November 3, 1954. For several minutes after putting down the telephone, Pablo could not speak.

He felt great sorrow and remorse. Matisse's talent, he knew, was as great or perhaps greater than his own. But Pablo had never fully expressed his admiration to Matisse. Now it was too late.

Matisse's death, however, triggered a new surge of energy in Pablo. In December, with a regular domestic life restored, Pablo started a series of paintings based on *Women of Algiers* by the nineteenth-century French master Ferdinand-Victor-Eugène Delacroix. The full-bosomed harem women, with their supple bodies and colorful surroundings, had been a favorite theme for Matisse, who had had such success with it that he more or less claimed Delacroix's painting as his own. With Matisse dead, however, Pablo decided that the way was open for his own treatment of harem women.

His series even followed some Matisse traits of style, including bolder use of color and more emphasis on pattern. It seemed that Pablo was trying to bring Matisse back to life. Actually, he was using Matisse in the same way as he used the old masters. They helped his own artistic growth. The harem paintings were a true tribute.

19

LIFE WITH JACQUELINE

While Jacqueline took charge at the studio, Pablo continued working on his *Women of Algiers* series. He put Delacroix's composition through many variations—moving, sometimes deleting, figures. He changed colors as well as forms. In some paintings, he used geometric shapes with hard angles to describe the figures. In others, full-bodied volumes with sweeping lines dominated.

Each painting in the series was distinctly different. Each carried a different mood. Indeed, it is difficult to believe that all shared the same inspiration. But all have the Picasso touch. Where Delacroix had created serenity, sensuality, and charm in a romantic setting, Pablo's pictures were alive with implied motion, vivid colors, and tense sexuality.

He worked on the *Women of Algiers* series from December 13, 1954, until February 14, 1955, producing a total of fifteen oils. During the same industrious period, he also produced two lithographs based on the Delacroix theme. Although there seems to be little to link the series together, many critics see it as a kind of review of all of Picasso's styles. Indeed, it seems as if Pablo wanted to test all his approaches against Delacroix's.

Some have described the Delacroix series as an homage to love, inspired this time by Jacqueline. Her face not only appears several times in the pictures, but while working on the series, he also did several portraits of her dressed in Arabian costumes. These were done with a full range of colors reminiscent of Matisse as much as of Delacroix.

Not long after they were completed, the paintings were exhibited in Germany, where an American collector saw them and bought all fifteen of them. An amused Pablo said it was too many women for one man to have. And, indeed, the collection was soon split up among several American buyers.

Although the series helped rekindle Pablo's creative energy, Jacqueline saw to it that he did not waste his talents. Pablo, to her, was both a lover and a responsibility. She shielded him from unwelcome visitors and other distractions. She provided a calm atmosphere that allowed Pablo's imagination to grow and expand. Her attention and devotion were exactly what the seventy-three-year-old artist needed.

On February 11, 1955, Olga Picasso died. She was buried in a quiet ceremony. Soon after attending the funeral, Pablo and Jacqueline thought about returning to the Riviera. They did not know exactly where they would live. They both had strong ties with Vallauris, but for Pablo, Villa la Galloise carried too many reminders of Françoise.

They took rooms in a hotel in Cannes not far from Vallauris. Dor de La Souchère, curator of the Antibes museum, was one of their first visitors. He invited them to come to the museum, but Pablo declined. He did not want to be reminded of Françoise, who had influenced his work so strongly when he was painting the big panels.

They began house hunting. Collecting property had become a kind of obsession with Pablo. Property seemed to fill a need for security, a need that may have had its roots in his early years of poverty. Now, although he might not use a home or studio for years, he refused to give it up. The home on rue de la Boétie in Paris, where he and Olga had spent the first years of marriage and where Paulo was born, remained in Pablo's hands, virtually unused. In 1951, however, because of the severe housing shortage in Paris, the French government had forced him to give it up.

The new home that he and Jacqueline acquired was a large and ornate villa above Cannes. It was called La Californie. Unlike the house in Vallauris, the villa at Cannes was surrounded by a garden with eucalyptus and mimosa trees and a high fence. The front gate of the villa was soon manned by a watchman. His orders were to say to all but a few friends that Pablo and Jacqueline were out.

This policy still allowed plenty of visits from friends and celebrities. The Western movie actor Gary Cooper came with his family and delighted Pablo with the gifts of a large cowboy hat and a pistol.

Pablo could be very sentimental about friends from the early days. He said there would always be a room in his house for Braque. He felt the same about Sabartés, Kahnweiler, the Leirises, Pallarés, and many others. He might at times heap verbal abuse on these people behind their backs, but that didn't reflect his seemingly true affection. He loved to tease Jean Cocteau to his face by repeatedly interrupting his long discourses, but Cocteau was always welcomed warmly at La Californie.

Pablo was not so sentimental about his women friends. When Fernande Olivier, his great passion of the bohemian days, was reported ill and destitute, Pablo sent money to her only after much grumbling. He commented that Braque was in a better position to help her.

Marie-Thérèse Walter's only recent hold on Pablo had been through Maya. Even this link eventually weakened when Maya married a naval officer. For years, Marie-Thérèse did not know what her future would hold. Pablo misled her without mercy.

At first Claude and Paloma, Françoise's children, visited La Californie frequently. They were good companions for Jacqueline's daughter, Cathy. Pablo played with the children and painted them often. Maya and Juan, Inez's son, sometimes joined the household, and Paulo was a frequent visitor. There were many happy afternoons spent on the warm beach. Later, visits from the children were discouraged. Only Paulo, the one legitimate child, could be sure of a welcome.

The insulation Jacqueline provided fit Pablo's needs perfectly. He had always worked in horror of the unexpected interruption. His greatest fear during the Nazi occupation of Paris was not physical harm to himself or his friends but fear that his work would be interrupted.

There were two important Picasso shows in Paris in 1955. One, a retrospective show, had 150 works ranging from his early days to the present. The other featured prints that Pablo had done over a period of almost fifty years. The show included many of the etchings and lithographs he had done for book illustrations.

There were many other shows in Europe and America, and 1955 brought the publication of still more Picasso books. No living artist was ever so well documented. Meanwhile, Christian Zervos continued to bring out supplements to his monumental catalogue depicting and describing each of Pablo's works.

The summer of 1955 was a particularly hot one for the south of France, but that did not stop Pablo from making a film. Director Henri-Georges Clouzot, who had been discussing the project off and on with Pablo for years, wanted to explore the creative process. What could be better than showing the world's most famous artist at work? Clouzot, himself famous as a director, employed a cameraman named Claude Renoir, grandson of the renowned painter.

Something more than talent, however, would be needed to capture creativity on film. For several years, Pablo found excuses to avoid the project, but then he made a discovery with a highly intense ink. When he brushed the ink on paper, the image showed through on the back side just as black as it was on the front. Pablo immediately called Clouzot, and the director grasped the possibilities at once.

With the camera on Pablo at a low angle, both the artist and his work as it appeared on the paper could be captured on film. This low angle was used for a large part of the film. Pablo also worked on a big canvas, a beach scene he called *La Garoupe*. When working on this, a more conventional, over-the-shoulder angle was used.

Pablo found filmmaking difficult. Close-ups and frequent changes of camera position interfered with his work. He could not paint at his usual pace. He wanted to take an idea and see it through to the finish without having to stop every few minutes for a new angle or a rest period for the crew. Often he ignored the order to "cut" and went right on working. If Renoir still had film, he continued shooting.

Clouzot and his crew were amazed at Pablo's capacity for work. The heat did not seem to bother him. When forced to take a break, Pablo moved to a nearby easel, where he worked on drawings.

On the final day of shooting, however, he collapsed. He might have fallen to the ground, had not one of the crew caught him. Jacqueline made him rest for several weeks. He saw no one and did no work. Meanwhile, Clouzot was busy in Paris editing his film.

Le Mystère Picasso was not the director's greatest film. It revealed no mystery and showed the creative process as little more than hard work. But Clouzot's movie is the only one that captured Pablo at work. The film, shown from time to time on American television, is still fascinating.

Although Jacqueline controlled the schedule, she let Pablo do pretty much what he wanted with the villa. He had never had so much space. As room after room filled up with the typical Picasso clutter, he gradually claimed the whole house as his studio. Long-forgotten trappings from the house and studio at rue la Boétie had to be shipped to La Californie. Sabartés, still serving as Pablo's Paris business manager, supervised the shipping. He also sent whatever paintings and supplies Pablo requested from the studio at rue des Grands-Augustins. Sabartés occasionally visited La Californie, but most of his time was divided between Paris and Barcelona.

In addition to being a curiosity shop, La Californie was also a menagerie. There were three dogs: a dachshund, a dalmation, and a boxer; and a goat named Esmeralda. She lived in the second-floor hallway. Pigeons lived on the third floor.

Furniture was sparse. Beds, chairs, tables, and a bureau or two were tolerated. It was an interior decorator's nightmare. The clutter, statues, and paintings were arranged at random. Bullfighting posters hung beside African masks. But the garden was more orderly. Pablo placed several bronze castings in the garden with great care. *Pregnant Woman, Man with the Sheep, Baboon with Young,* and *She-Goat* graced the shade of the eucalyptus and mimosa trees to charming advantage.

Pablo dressed meticulously. Although he wore some wild things, he always selected them with great attention to color and cut. He wanted his trousers to fit perfectly and match or complement his shirts.

An Italian tailor in nearby Nice, by the name of Sapone, was a frequent visitor at La Californie. The man knew

Pablo's needs and worked hard to please him. Eventually, Sapone made trips to Italy, Greece, and Yugoslavia to get the woolens and corduroys that Pablo liked. Pablo, who paid for this service with paintings, made Sapone one of the wealthiest men in his trade, and he was one of the few who could gain admittance to La Californie unannounced.

One morning, the filmmaker Vladimir Pozner came to La Californie to claim the drawing that Pablo had promised for a poster. The poster was to advertise *Song of the Rivers,* a film dealing with workers of all races. Pablo had not done the drawing, nor had he given it much thought, but while Pozner watched, Pablo began developing an idea. He started with four hands of different colors, grouped in a circle like the petals of a flower. After five hours and twenty-one sketches, Pablo finally handed a finished drawing to the filmmaker. When Pozner, amazed at Pablo's extended focus of energy, thanked him, Pablo said no thanks was necessary. He had only done what was asked.

At this time, in addition to innumerable portraits of Jacqueline, Pablo also began painting interiors of each room in the villa. In this way, he took stock of the unopened crates, scattered tools, canvas stretchers, stored paintings, and junk that filled each space. The series also gave Pablo the satisfaction of ownership. Each painting laid claim to the room it depicted.

The interiors sometimes had more to say about his moods than the room itself. Somber canvases in the series may have related to the spring of 1955, which was unusually stormy. There were others, however, that danced with enough Oriental patterns and colors to suggest Matisse paintings. Sometimes he showed Jacqueline standing or sitting amid the clutter. He completed the last interior in June 1956. He felt now that he owned La Californie both legally and spiritually.

He next moved into the garden for inspiration. There were many sketches of insects. In a whimsical mood, he showed a bull climbing up a flower stem like a grasshopper seeking the sun.

In this period, he often preferred doing portraits in a series of sketches rather than as one oil painting. When the poet Jacques Prévert came for a visit, Pablo spent twenty-one days doing twenty-six drawings. He had a similar response to a visit from the pianist Arthur Rubinstein, except this time he did twenty-one portraits in just a few hours. Some of these drawings where little more than energetic scribbles, but to Pablo they were all likenesses.

Celebrations of Picasso's seventy-fifth year began well before the actual event. Honors flowed in from governments, and congratulations came from individuals. There were shows everywhere. Pablo loved the daily arrival of the mail. There were always letters from friends. Sabartés wrote almost daily. He also enjoyed some of the many letters that now came from strangers. Most people wrote to praise some particular work, but a few criticized something. Others asked about his Communist beliefs. Newspapers and magazines never stopped asking for interviews. Pablo granted very few, but he loved reading the papers, even the small weeklies.

Although Pablo had vowed not to set foot in his native Spain as long as Franco remained in charge, he was delighted to hear that his work would be shown in Barcelona. This would help maintain his Spanish connections. Sabartés had made the arrangements for a yearly Picasso exhibit in a Barcelona gallery, one of the best in Spain.

The first show was held in October of 1956. Others followed each fall, showing recent work that Pablo himself selected. Later, he agreed to provide work for a show in his native Málaga, to be held in the summer of 1957.

When October 25, the day of his seventy-fifth birthday arrived, Pablo and Jacqueline, with Jean Cocteau, went to the Ramiés' pottery shop to celebrate. There was a seventy-five-pound cake with seventy-five candles. Pablo blew them out with three big breaths. The pottery workers applauded and gave him a copper potter's wheel. Georges Ramié made a speech. Pablo thanked everyone, returned to La Californie, and went back to work.

A month later, a major Picasso show opened in Moscow. The Communist press, now leery of Picasso's art, made little mention of the show, but it was a great success. Attendance held at three thousand or more people a day throughout.

Conservative party leaders, however, criticized the works as degenerate. This blocked further showings of Pablo's art in Russia for the next ten years.

But attitudes toward communism changed in the 1950s. Revelations of the despotism and cruelty of Stalin had come to light. And it was during Pablo's Moscow show that Soviet soldiers crushed Hungary's hopes for freedom. A liberalizing movement in Poland was also squelched. Many who, out of idealism, had joined the Communist party became disillusioned. Some of Pablo's friends publicly tore up their party membership cards. Pablo himself joined nine other intellectuals in signing a letter to the central committee calling for a special party convention to resolve "burning questions of conscience." Although the letter was leaked to the press, the party did not react. Some Communists feared Pablo might withdraw from the party. He did not, but his interest in politics had definitely waned.

A Seventy-Fifth Anniversary Picasso Exhibition opened in May 1957 in New York's Museum of Modern Art. Later, it moved on to Chicago and then Philadelphia. There was also a major Picasso exhibit at Arles, in southern France.

By now, Pablo had produced so many paintings, sculptures, pottery, and prints that several exhibits could easily be held simultaneously, and almost every museum that valued its reputation now had some Picassos in its permanent collection. Meanwhile, Pablo continued producing at the same remarkable pace.

In the summer of 1957, Pablo turned to his countryman Diego Velázquez, the seventeenth-century painter, for inspiration. Using that master's *Las Meninas* as a starting point, Pablo did a series of fifty-eight paintings. And, while working on this major project, he began sketches for a mural that had been commissioned for the UNESCO building in Paris.

Most men his age had been retired for ten years. Pablo, however, did not seem to know what retirement meant.

20

BIG WORKS

Velázquez's *Las Meninas* is a complex, provocative painting. It is not at once apparent that the artist used
reflections to show all members of the royal family, and that
he did it to explore different levels of reality.

The king and queen of Spain appear in a small mirror at
the back of a large room. In the foreground are the young
ladies of the court. They are with a dog and a dwarf. Behind
them are two attendants. Almost all are looking out at the
viewer, including Velázquez himself, who stands, brush in
hand. What is he studying so intently? It takes a moment to
realize that he is looking into a mirror. With this realization,
the viewer finally understands that the entire scene is a
reflection. At least, Velázquez intended it to appear so.

Here was a favorite Picasso theme, the artist in his studio,
done by one of his favorite old masters. But perhaps even

more fascinating to Pablo was the way Velázquez was dealing with the Spanish court. The life of the Spanish royalty was in a dreamworld far removed from the struggle and poverty of most people in Spain three centuries ago.

Velázquez, by using reflections, emphasized the artificial nature of court life, a life that he himself benefited from and enjoyed. Perhaps this is why he put himself in the picture. Or does his presence represent another level of reality? The puzzle fascinated Pablo.

Pablo approached his Velázquez series with great intensity. He demanded complete silence in the house when he was at work. Gloom descended on La Californie. The summer of 1957 was difficult. Jacqueline was recuperating at the time from an operation. Picasso himself suffered from a chronic pain in his leg, which often could not be ignored.

Visits from all but a few friends were not allowed. Pablo would see the Pignons, the Leirises, Kahnweiler, Sabartés, and his favorite photographer, David Duncan Douglas, but all others were told to call back later. Pablo had to concentrate. Even when he wasn't working, he needed to think about the project.

He did put his brushes aside for the bullfights, but even on these outings, friends recalled, Pablo was not his usual self. He was too preoccupied to enjoy fully the festivities and the company.

For the first painting in the series, he chose a large seventy-seven-by-ninety-five-inch canvas and a blue-gray palette. He included all the elements of Velázquez's composition, but he distorted and simplified the figures beyond recognition. Pablo turned Velázquez himself into something that looked more like an Indian totem than an artist at his canvas.

Before attempting another full rendition, Pablo did nineteen studies of the *infanta,* or youngest, of the royal daughters. In some of these, he used childlike lines to separate what

209

he saw as the drawn parts from the painted parts of the original. His main goal was to take the masterpiece apart to show what made it work.

For the rest of 1957, he did little work not connected with *Las Meninas.* The only exceptions were sketches for the UNESCO project, some paintings of pigeons, a few landscapes, and a portrait of Jacqueline. His last painting of the year depicted the infanta in green-gray harmony, highlighted with rose.

The UNESCO mural demanded more of his time in 1958, but he continued to work on the Velázquez series with the same intensity. He showed the canvases to no one, and his few visitors grew tired of hearing about work they never saw. Pablo toyed with their curiosity until the day he was finished. Even then, he played games. He had Jacqueline invite a few overnight guests to La Californie. It was Sunday, October 6, 1958.

The work was on the third floor, but Pablo did not take any of the guests upstairs, not right away. He only hinted that they might see the work that evening, but talk over dinner lasted far into the night. The Leirises went to bed. Finally, in the early morning hours, Pablo took Édouard Pignon to the third floor. His wife, who was not invited, spent two sleepless hours waiting for her husband to return. When he did, he spent the rest of the night describing Pablo's Velázquez series to her.

Pignon repeated the description for the other guests the next morning while Pablo continued to play his teasing game. Finally, however, he took everyone up to the third floor, where the entire series of fifty-eight canvases was viewed one by one. The silent appreciation that greeted the work made Pablo grin broadly. It was a most satisfactory unveiling.

For public viewing, the collection traveled from Galerie Louise Leiris in Paris to the Tate Gallery in London. There were several other showings before Pablo donated all fifty-eight canvases to the Museo Picasso in Barcelona, soon after it was established.

Meanwhile, Pablo had completed and exhibited the huge painting for the UNESCO delegates lounge. Like much commissioned work, it had given him trouble. At first, he had refused to accept the job, saying it should go to a younger man. He had pointed out that he was now seventy-six, but George Salles, unofficial minister of French museums, had persuaded him to change his mind.

Size alone presented problems. The painting, to cover a high wall of the lounge, was to be done on dozens of wooden panels two meters square, which would be assembled at the site. As usual, Pablo started with innumerable sketches, some in pencil, others in ink or colored pencil. He first depicted a studio interior with a painter and a reclining model as main figures. This idea gradually evolved into something else. Bathers and a diver appeared in later drawings. Then the reclining model reappeared. The scene began to look like a gathering at a swimming pool.

Pablo was not satisfied. Furthermore, he was behind schedule. Early in 1958, he had scrapped his original idea and started over. Friends said he was influenced by *Sputnik*, the first artificial earth satellite launched by the Soviet Union. Whatever the influence, the new sketches were different, and Pablo was at last satisfied.

Translating the sketch onto the wooden panels was extremely difficult. Pablo could find no building on the Riviera large enough to hold the assembled work. He could put together only small sections in La Californie. When he finished a panel, Jacqueline would place it in the proper position next to the other completed panels. He could make changes to assure that the panel fit with its immediate neighbors but he could only guess how the fully assembled work would look.

211

Meanwhile, UNESCO officials began to worry. Pablo had shown his sketches to no one, not even the architect. Was he making any progress at all? The question began to appear in critical newspaper and magazine articles. How could Pablo create a mural for a building he had never seen? How could something so big be painted in a small studio?

Pablo at first ignored the articles, but eventually he decided something must be done. He unveiled the painting, fully assembled, in a Vallauris school yard.

The ceremonies, a big event for the small town, were held on March 29, 1958. Many UNESCO dignitaries and other officials came from Paris. There were also several reporters. The townspeople and Pablo's friends applauded the work warmly the moment it was unveiled. The UNESCO representatives, however, were cool. Within hours, critical articles appeared in Paris newspapers. Communist papers attacked the work as another abstraction that would have to be explained to the workers.

Pablo's own confidence had been slightly shaken when the painting was first unveiled. The harsh sunlight was not kind to the cool blues and greens. Later, in the soft light of evening, however, the painting came to life. Pablo was satisfied. Perhaps his friends were right. He had created another masterpiece.

It was Georges Salles, Director of the Louvre, who named the work *The Fall of Icarus*. This satisfied the critics, who could now explain the painting as an illustration from mythology. It showed the Greek hero whose wings, put together with wax, melted when he flew too close to the sun. Pablo, however, insisted that he had had nothing so specific in mind when he had created the mural. He always referred to it as his UNESCO painting.

At a banquet to dedicate the building, there was much debate among Paris officials over the meaning of Pablo's work. He was not there, but toward the end of the evening,

Le Corbusier, a world-renowned architect, spoke in praise of the work. He said it was a masterpiece and, like all masterpieces, it could not be easily explained. Le Corbusier then suggested that a telegram be sent to Picasso, congratulating him on the achievement. Despite some grumbling, the telegram was sent.

Icarus resembled Matisse's colorful cutouts. Indeed, Matisse had made a cutout, later reproduced as a lithograph, on the Icarus theme. Pablo might well have had his rival in mind. Soon after finishing the UNESCO painting, he began making cutouts of his own.

These, however, were not made with papers of various colors to be pasted up in a collage as Matisse had done. Pablo's restless and inventive mind had to find a new approach. He used scissors to cut shapes from sheets of cardboard. The shapes were later folded and fitted with other shapes to become freestanding, three-dimensional images of animals and people.

The structures that pleased him were later recreated in metal by a craftsman who used the cardboard as patterns. Various textures and thicknesses of metal were used, and Pablo then added further variety by painting selected parts of the work. In this way, he created a new series of sculptures.

Sales of Picassos continued at a brisk pace. In 1957 alone, Kahnweiler, dealing out of the Galerie Louise Leiris in Paris, sold seventy Picassos, for a total of $1,200,000. And the volume and the prices would increase with each year. Perhaps it was this ever-increasing wealth that encouraged Pablo to buy another home.

It was in September of 1958 that friends suggested he take a look at the seven-hundred-year-old château de Vauvenargues near Aix-en-Provence. Once the estate of an aristocratic family, the place was several miles to the west of Cannes and well inland from the coast. Pablo was keenly interested. The château stood in the center of Cézanne country. In fact, the big building, with its flanking towers, rose on a rocky prominence on the side of Montagne Sainte-Victoire, the mountain that Cézanne had made famous in his many landscapes.

Jacqueline thought the place was spooky. It was an austere building surrounded by fourteenth-century fortifications and backed by dark oaks, pines, and cypress. The body of Saint Severin was buried under one of the towers. Pablo thought the château looked like a Spanish castle.

Although there was no central heating, the large, spacious rooms of the château convinced Pablo that he must have it. Jacqueline, not at all enthusiastic about moving, made Pablo promise to keep La Californie. He could agree easily. He had no intention of selling it.

Pablo bought the château for $120,000 and put up another $50,000 for improvements, including central heating. The work took almost a year. Meanwhile, he sent crates of paintings and studio gear to the château. His collection came out of storage. Soon the works of Braque, Matisse, Cézanne, and many other painters hung on the château walls. Some works had been in storage so long that Pablo had almost forgotten them. He was delighted to feast his eyes again.

He and Jacqueline moved to Vauvenargues in February 1959. It was impossible to furnish every room, but Jacqueline installed several pieces of large furniture with the hope of making some of the vast rooms seem livable. Pablo had selected an old, rather ugly buffet as his contribution. The buffet was to appear frequently in his paintings of that period.

Because of Jacqueline's distaste for it, the château did not become a permanent residence. Pablo found it hard to adjust to the new surroundings, and Jacqueline could not get back to La Californie soon enough. Just the same, Pablo managed to work in the château. He filled dozens of sketch pads with bullfight scenes, women washing their feet, heads, nudes, and centaurs. His paintings entered a very colorful phase. He switched from oils to enamels to produce glossy colors.

One painting from this period shows a women reading in a bright cone of light. The composition for *Woman Beneath the Lamp* would later be used for a linoleum-block print Pablo called *Still Life Beneath the Lamp.*

Pablo's interest in cutting linoleum broadened the dimensions of the technique. Because of its carving ease and economy, printing from linoleum blocks had been identified as a craft for school children. It was a restricted medium. Details and subtle shifts of values were not possible, but Pablo saw the restrictions as a challenge.

Although he had done some linoleum prints in the 1930s, he had been diverted for many years by lithography, etching, and other more sophisticated printing techniques. In Vallauris, however, he met a linoleum craftsman by the name of Arnera, who had a poster shop that Pablo had first visited in 1954. Pablo drew both inspiration and instruction from Arnera, who had learned the craft from his father.

Pablo's experiments soon led him to a new method of printing several colors from one block. He summoned Arnera to La Californie one day to show him how it worked. In this method, now known as the reduction method, the uncarved block is first printed in a light color. While carefully registering each print, enough impressions are taken to fill the desired number of an edition—ten, twenty, or however many there might be. Then part of the block is carved. A darker color is used for the second printing, so that the original, light color will appear only where the block has been carved. Although this process can continue through a dozen or more colors, Pablo rarely used more than three colors.

He did a series of prints using ochers, browns, and blacks. Later, he used whites, greens, and blues. Over a period of eight years, Pablo did bullfight scenes, bacchanals, portraits

215

of Jacqueline, guitar players, still lifes, and interiors. Pablo easily overcame the limitations of the technique and raised the humble linocut to a respected medium.

Another innovation only Pablo could have pioneered was a method of achieving thin, dark lines with linoleum. Normally, making thin lines is tedious because the artist must carefully cut away material on either side of the line. Pablo reversed the entire concept of the block print. He used a thin gouge to cut thin lines into the block. These lines, uninked, would normally have shown as white lines in the print, but Pablo, instead of printing with black ink on white paper, printed with white ink on black paper. Where he had made his cuts, black lines thus appeared.

It was a simple solution, but it seems that Pablo was the first to discover it. He did not use it often, however, because he was more interested in the bold shapes of the linoleum prints. For line work, he could always resort to etchings or engravings.

The work with linoleum influenced his paintings, which soon had more emphasis on shapes and less emphasis on detail.

On August 10, 1959, at Vauvenargues, Pablo started the preliminary sketches for a new cycle of paintings. These would be based on Édouard Manet's *Luncheon on the Grass*, which shows two clothed men having a picnic in a park with a seated, naked woman, as a partially clad woman wades in a background stream. The large painting scandalized Paris when it was first shown there in 1863.

Of course, the scandal appealed to Pablo, but he also recognized an old theme. Manet's *Luncheon on the Grass* was once again simply the artist and his model in an outdoor setting.

In two and a half years, Pablo did 138 drawings, 28 paintings, and some linoleum cuts based on the Manet. This was a much bigger, more prolonged project than Pablo's previous works based on the Delacroix and Velázquez masterpieces, but Manet held a special fascination for him. He was a pioneer of modern art and a great influence in his day on younger painters, including Cézanne and others who had influenced Pablo.

By the time Pablo finished his *Luncheon on the Grass* cycle, he had passed his eightieth birthday. He had worked on many other projects during the Manet cycle. Sculptures based on his cardboard cutouts, more ceramics, many sketches of bullfights, and his prints had kept him as busy as ever. He also had found time to do some work based on Rembrandt's *Bathsheba*.

Many special exhibits around the world were held to mark his eightieth year. Pablo, however, could generate little interest in them. The exhibits all represented past work, past achievements. He now was far more interested in the future, the work and the achievement that were still to come. His advancing years gave urgency to his efforts. There was much still to be done. Would there be time?

Although he could ignore most shows and honors, he was most vitally interested in having his work appreciated in Spain. There, popular enthusiasm for Picasso was gradually softening government resistance.

For some time, Sabartés had been urging the establishment of a Picasso museum in Barcelona. When the improved political climate made this idea seem something more than a dream, other old friends gave their support. Many came to La Californie or Vauvenargues to discuss the project with Pablo. He was skeptical. Didn't he still represent the freedom that Franco denied his countrymen? Wasn't the regime still afraid of him?

There indeed was resistance, but it was centered mostly in Madrid. The citizens of Barcelona wanted a museum for Spain's most famous living artist. The annual Picasso shows had already prepared the city for his art. Attendance and sales had risen with each show until they had become a major cultural event of the year.

Just the same, much patience and diplomacy were needed to overcome government resistance. Eventually, the proposal was put before Franco himself. Fortunately, Franco at the time was in need of certain political backing from Barcelona. He signed the necessary papers without protest.

The leaders of the project quickly acquired and refurbished an old mansion. Pablo gave a generous collection of his work, including many early paintings and sketches that had never before been exhibited. Later, Pablo would give many more paintings and drawings to the museum. Sabartés donated his substantial collection of Picassos as a bequest.

While the museum was taking shape without serious protest, the liberal faction of the city put the political climate to a test. Xavier Busquets, who had built Barcelona's new College of Architecture, asked Pablo to decorate the cement walls with sandblasted murals. Pablo agreed, and the news brought a deluge of objections. The college stood across the street from the Barcelona cathedral. Pablo's design would thus be in full view of the city's most conservative citizens.

The archbishop had already blessed the walls of the college, never suspecting that those walls would soon bear the art of a Communist. Again, however, popular support overrode objections and the project won approval. Pablo adopted a style of primitive art based on Spain's archeological relics. The general theme was a street festival, and although the murals are far short of his best work, they remain the pride of Barcelona.

21

MARRIED AGAIN

Pablo Picasso and Jacqueline Roque were married on March 2, 1961. They told no one of their plans. They simply went into the office of the mayor of Vallauris, and the mayor married them while a notary and his wife served as witnesses. Back at La Californie, the newlyweds broke the news to their surprised servants, poured champagne for all, and laughed over their adventure.

Why the secrecy? Even Paulo had been kept in the dark. He learned about the wedding by reading the papers like everyone else. Many friends thought that Jacqueline had insisted on privacy, but Pablo himself had certainly grown weary by now of the public spotlight.

Soon after the wedding, Pablo and Jacqueline had a restless urge to relocate. New houses, even apartment buildings, were cropping up at an alarming pace around La Californie.

They felt hemmed in. Jacqueline would not agree to live full-time at Vauvenargues, so they began house hunting again.

They found an estate on a hilltop in Mougins, a few miles northwest of Vallauris. Pablo had spent three summers in Mougins with Dora Maar and the Éluards in the late 1930s. Then he had stayed in a hotel. Now he would live in a grand estate.

It was called Notre-Dame-de-Vie and included a cemetery and a small three-hundred-year-old chapel dedicated to "Our Lady of Life." The main building was shielded from the street by an olive grove and a row of cypress. The building was tall enough, however, to give a magnificent view of château towers, village rooftops, and the distant waters of the Mediterranean. For Pablo, the best feature was the building's endless rooms. They were large and airy—perfect studios.

Eventually, Pablo would use up even this space and have to add a new wing on the back of the building, but he was content to spend his final, highly productive years in Mougins.

The routine was soon established at the new residence. Days and evenings were devoted to work. A select group of visitors was welcome in the late afternoon.

People who could revive old memories delighted Pablo. Serge Lifar, a star of the Ballets Russes in the 1920s, appeared one day with many fond recollections and a request for help. He asked Pablo for an illustration for an album of his famous dances. Pablo quickly did a drawing and a portrait. Later, when Lifar became master of the Paris Opera, he asked Pablo to do a drop curtain for *Afternoon of a Faun.* Pablo's horned faun chasing a frightened nymph was apparently too erotic for Lifar's conservative boss. It was not used in Paris, but the curtain was used in Toulouse when the ballet was performed there in 1965.

Meanwhile, a set design for Lifar's *Icarus,* reminiscent of his UNESCO mural, was accepted in 1962 without protest. It was the last work Pablo did for the theater.

Notre-Dame-de-Vie, as might be expected, was soon cluttered. Large ceramic pieces and metal sculptures crowded the main hall, and there were paintings everywhere. But the house was quiet. Pablo worked without distraction.

A shop for the Crommelinck brothers, Aldo and Pietro, who now printed Pablo's etchings and engravings, was set up in the town of Mougins. Pablo constantly sent them new plates for edition printings. And he continued to draw, paint, and sculpt.

When he did rest from his labors, he watched television. The fast-changing images fascinated him. Sometimes he practiced drawing by turning the sound off and sketching images as they came on the screen. With television to amuse him, Jacqueline to care for him, and her carefully picked group to flatter him, he could ask for little more.

He still went to bullfights, but these were now quiet excursions. There was no train of admirers, no fanfare. Pablo wanted to savor the dignity and solemnity of the old ritual of the ring. Often he sat in the stands with no one but Jacqueline and his chauffeur.

Some old friends who were denied access to Pablo blamed Jacqueline and spread unfair gossip about her. But she was a devoted wife. Preserving the privacy of a world celebrity was no easy job. She was bound to offend some people.

Perhaps Pablo might have produced diligently without Jacqueline's help. His most common complaint at this time was that he still had much to say and not enough time left to say it, but the stability Jacqueline provided certainly made work easier for him.

Early in February of 1963, he completed an antiwar painting showing two warriors, one on horseback, fighting above a shrieking woman and child who are being crushed in the melee. To give it a classical reference, Pablo called it *The*

Rape of the Sabine Woman, but it was closer in style and content to *Guernica* than to Greek or Roman times.

He followed this picture with scores of other scenes depicting fighting and massacres, always showing the victims as helpless and innocent creatures. His helmeted warriors did indeed look classical, but bullfight references were also obvious in most of the paintings.

He seemed to paint with the same facility as always, but he told Hélène Parmelin during the height of this phase that it was the most difficult painting he had ever attempted.

He filled studio after studio with battle paintings, but by the spring of 1963 they began to give way to the old theme of the painter in his studio. Although the style was now looser, more impetuous, the spirit of these studio paintings echoed the studio interiors he had done for the *Vollard Suite* back in the 1930s.

Again, he wanted to probe the creative process. He concentrated fully for almost two months on this theme, but he could not exclude the outside world entirely.

Braque was terminally ill, and Pablo thought of him often until the end, which came on August 31, 1963. Pablo watched the funeral on television and later invited Braque's widow for a visit at Notre-Dame-de-Vie. Two other old friends, Cocteau and Sabartés, were ill. Fernande Olivier was living alone in poverty and poor health.

The Museo Picasso in Barcelona had opened on March 10, 1963. Because of the political climate, there was no ceremony. The building did not even have a sign. Sabartés saw these omissions as calculated insults and refused to go to the museum on opening day.

Picasso was not so easily upset. His work demanded all his energy and emotion. In October, he began etching again. In rapid succession, he turned out three copper plates, each dealing with a couple embracing. Next came a plate showing a painter at work. This was soon followed with a sculptor in his studio. Then came a plate showing art collectors gazing at an abstract sculpture, while a seductive model watches from an armchair. Everyone was, of course, shown nude.

His plate production was to keep Aldo and Pietro Crommelinck busy in their print shop until the spring of 1964, when Pablo put aside copper plates for a few months to concentrate again on painting.

In January 1964, the Galerie Louise Leiris in Paris held a Picasso show that included sixty-eight recent paintings completed during the previous thirteen months. The show quieted any rumors that Pablo had slowed down. He was not only producing a great volume of work, but he was still experimenting as inventively as ever.

He borrowed from the movies to use sequences to show how an idea or an image might change from one painting to the next. At the same time, he also painted scores of heads, using "models" that were stored in his memory. He drew heavily on his past for ideas and styles, but his paintings were fresh and spontaneous. There was often a sketchiness in his work that suggested that he was in a hurry to get everything down.

Pablo told his old friend Pignon that he now resented the loss of a day from his studio.

He sometimes varied the artist and his model theme by replacing the artist with a man smoking. He almost always worked out these compositions as sketches before taking up his brush and palette. In another variation, he sometimes showed the artist, often a pathetic figure, facing a blank canvas. A blank canvas, Pablo believed, was the most terrifying thing in an artist's life.

In the summer of 1964, he returned to etching, using the tonal technique of aquatint and colored inks to continue the theme of a man smoking. The Crommelincks were busy again, and Pablo kept their press turning well into 1965. That spring, however, he received an emotional jolt.

The French edition of Françoise Gilot's book *My Life with Picasso* was published with much fanfare. Françoise had written the book with journalist Carlton Lake, who had previously interviewed Pablo several times for newspapers and magazines. Although it generally was a fair account, it sometimes put Pablo in a bad light. Certain passages made him seem either petty, childish, or cruel. Pablo was dismayed. His friends saw the book as Françoise's revenge.

Actually, if Pablo had left things alone, the affair would not have become so painful. The English edition of the book, published the year before, had been praised for its insights into the great painter's personal life and creative methods. It had not caused much commotion.

Reaction to the French edition also seemed mild, but then Pablo sued to suppress it. The suit was a hopeless gesture and made Pablo seem pitiful even to some of his loyal fans. The lawsuit failed, but it focused enough public attention on the book to turn it into a best-seller.

It was a sad episode. Pablo stoutly maintained that he had never read the book. It seemed for a time that he was the only person in France who had not. He forbade mention of Françoise's name. Claude and Paloma found that Pablo would not see them. The children reminded him of Françoise. He took refuge in the studio, where his mood found expression. He painted in layers and blobs. He gouged and scraped into the thick pigment with angry strokes. He portrayed disjointed figures of nudes, fauns, smokers, and other figures all crushed together in crowded compositions. Jacqueline told friends that she was terrified by the work.

In the studio scenes, the figure of the painter was replaced by a musketeer. The musketeer's costume was suggested by the clothing of Rembrandt's day. Pablo had already drawn inspiration from Rembrandt's self-portraits. The musketeers he now painted, however, were swordsmen, not painters. By removing the painter from these studio scenes, Pablo was taking himself out of the picture. Was it an attempt to get a fresh look at the creative process, or was his removal a reaction to Françoise's book?

Later, influenced by a circus he had seen on television, Pablo returned to the acrobats, equestrians, and clowns that had peopled his rose period. By then, the angry strokes had given way to a calmer, more controlled style.

In the summer of 1965, Pablo was rumored to be in poor health. He was, after all, approaching his eighty-fourth birthday. And the fact was that his stomach had been bothering him for several weeks. He mentioned the problem to no one outside the family, and in mid-November, under great secrecy, he entered a Paris hospital for an ulcer operation. He was back at Mougins, recuperating, before most of his friends heard he had been sick. He recovered quickly and was soon at work again.

Meanwhile, with his eighty-fifth birthday now less than a year away, friends and fans began putting pressure on the French government for a major Picasso exhibition. It would be a retrospective show, including paintings, prints, and drawings that would represent all phases of Pablo's long career. French officials endorsed this idea publicly, but there was a problem. The government, led at this time by Charles de Gaulle, was fiercely anti-Communist. How could it honor the country's most famous Communist?

For a time, it seemed that the retrospective show would never come to pass.

André Malraux, the well-known novelist and war hero, was now minister of cultural affairs. He and Pablo had known each other since the Spanish civil war, when Malraux fought against Franco. Although they had once been friends, politics had drive them apart. Malraux feared that Pablo might use the exhibition to embarrass the de Gaulle regime.

For his part, Pablo did not trust Malraux, who had a reputation for unkept promises. Pablo also did not like the prospect of more publicity and the controversy that the show was sure to bring. Eventually, however, after learning that an old friend, Jean Leymarie, had been put in charge of the exhibition, he agreed to loan work for the show.

Leymarie was able to persuade officials that Picasso the artist was far more important than Picasso the Communist. It would an embarrassing oversight if France did not honor Picasso in his eighty-fifth year. The French government finally endorsed the project, but then another problem arose. The United States at the time was contesting de Gaulle's foreign policies. Many works that had to be borrowed for the exhibition were in museums in the United States. The museums were in no mood to cooperate with France.

Leymarie went to New York to visit an old friend. Alfred J. Barr, Jr., was now director of the Museum of Modern Art. If this museum loaned work to France, Leymarie correctly reasoned, the others would as well. Barr, a great Picasso fan and supporter, agreed to loan France everything Leymarie wanted except for *Guernica,* which was not in good enough condition to travel.

Other countries were quicker to show their generosity. Loans of major works came from Switzerland, Sweden, Holland, Czechoslovakia, and Russia. Leymarie had started with a goal of 100 paintings. Eventually he collected 284.

The show was to be staged in Paris's Grand Palais gallery, but Leymarie was determined to show Pablo's sculpture, most of which had never been exhibited before. The Grand Palais did not have room for both paintings and sculpture, so Leymarie took over the Petit Palais, another municipal gallery just across the street.

Pablo and Leymarie planned every room of the exhibition. No detail was overlooked. To Leymarie's disappointment, however, Pablo refused to go to Paris to supervise arrangements or attend the opening. Pablo did insist, however, on having photos of every wall in every exhibit room, and these were sent to him as the show took shape.

The opening was scheduled for November 19, 1966. Meanwhile, October 25, Pablo's birthday, came and went quietly. To avoid phone calls and visitors, he and Jacqueline stayed away from Notre-Dame-de-Vie most of the day. When they returned, friends were waiting with oysters and wine. They celebrated Pablo's eighty-fifth year with a light supper at the kitchen table.

The show opened to huge crowds. Reporters and art critics from around the world flocked to Paris. The reviews were mixed. As expected, ardent Picasso fans praised the show but most critics were puzzled and surprised. The artist had so many styles, moods, and techniques that it was difficult to write about him.

It was easiest to look at the many facets of Picasso's work one at a time. Some writers praised the beauty of his classical figures and condemned his ugly, disjointed forms. Others took an opposite view. It was hard for many to believe that the paintings of the blue and rose periods had been done by the same artist who produced cubist still lifes and grotesque heads that seemed to face two directions at the same time.

A London critic suggested that Pablo's facility might be a handicap. Because he could work in any style, he never settled comfortably into one way of working. After visiting the Petit Palais, some critics declared that Picasso was greater as a sculptor than as a painter.

Paris was not the only city to mark Pablo's birthday. There were major exhibits in Los Angeles, Dallas, Fort Worth, Basel, Lucerne, Barcelona, Prague, and Moscow. Smaller shows abounded. The commercial galleries of Paris seemed to bloom with Picassos.

Through it all, Pablo remained at home and worked, but he was not as indifferent to honors and praise as he pretended to be. When Hélène Parmelin returned to Mougins at midnight after attending the opening in Paris, she went straight to Notre-Dame-de-Vie. There, Pablo sat up in bed and listened avidly to her detailed description of the event.

Jean Leymarie hoped that the success of the show would convince the French government of the need for a Picasso museum in Paris. If a building were provided, Pablo had said he would donate a good body of work to France. With the price of important Picassos now set near the $250,000 level, it seemed to Leymarie and his associates that the government could not afford to miss the opportunity. But the government was not interested.

Pablo was bitter about the whole business. By 1970, the government had canceled his lease at rue des Grands-Augustins, and Bateau-Lavoir had burned down. He told friends that no trace of his long career in Paris remained.

Exhibitions and museums did not keep Pablo from his work. Etchings and engravings multiplied so rapidly that the Crommelinck brothers could not print the plates fast enough. Many plates from this period remained unprinted for several months.

The Crommelincks called Pablo's print production from this period his "logbook." In a way, Pablo treated each copper plate as if it were a page from a sketchbook. It was a way of recording each day's ideas and concerns. Many prints were erotic, showing men and women before, during, or after making love. Often the scenes included a watcher in the background, shown either as a musketeer, a bullfighter, or an aging artist.

Pablo produced 347 prints in one year alone, all on the same theme. There was a light, humorous spirit in these erotic prints. Later they became cruder, as Pablo's humor seemed to give way to a fascination with raw lust in all its perverse forms.

His paintings in this period included innumerable heads,

mostly portraits of Jacqueline, swordsmen, actors, bull-fighters, and musketeers. His strongest influence now was Rembrandt, but he still drew from other sources. He jokingly commented to a visitor that he copied everyone but himself, but this was not exactly true. He continued to draw on his own images and ideas from the past, often changing them almost beyond recognition.

He was working with the same, perhaps even more, intensity than ever before. By now, there were daily reminders of mortality.

22

THE FINAL YEARS

Sabartés died on February 13, 1968. The news jolted
Pablo. For several years, Jaime had written to him daily,
and Pablo had never failed to inscribe a proof of every one
of his prints to be sent to the old poet. Sabartés's death,
perhaps more than any other event, reminded Pablo that his
own end was near.

He began making generous donations. He gave 58 paintings in Jaime's memory to the Barcelona museum. Later,
through his lawyers, he arranged the transfer of all the early
works that his mother had preserved to the Barcelona museum. This did not please three nephews and a niece who had
hoped to inherit this collection. Pablo gave each of the relatives an oil painting and put them in charge of supervising
the transfer of the work, which included 103 paintings and
681 works on paper.

To house this added collection, Barcelona acquired another mansion next door to the existing Picasso museum. When installations in the new space were finished, Pablo received a stack of photographs showing how each work was displayed. His pictures revived memories of his bohemian days, the friends at the Four Cats, the good times, and the struggles of his youth.

Pablo gave his 1912 cubist *Guitar* to New York's Museum of Modern Art. He gave the same museum formal custody of *Guernica,* which it already had, with the understanding that the big painting would go to Spain when the Fascist regime ended.

By written bequest, he gave thirty-seven paintings from his collection of work by other artists and all of his African sculptures to the French government.

When Jean-Maurice Rouquette, director of the museum at Arles, asked for the loan of some recent work, Pablo would not at first commit himself. He and Jacqueline, however, invited Rouquette to Notre-Dame-de-Vie. There, the director described Arles's hopes for a new museum. Pablo still would not say if he would loan anything, but several weeks after his first visit, Rouquette was called back. Pablo had a surprise for him.

Pablo brought out three boxes full of recent drawings, and from them he, Jacqueline, and Rouquette selected fifty-seven drawings for the show. Then, as the director was gathering the work together, Pablo said he could consider them as a gift to the Arles museum. The director was nearly bowled over. Buying such a prize would have been possible only for a major museum.

For Pablo, the episode was one of the most gratifying of his long career. Generosity had been rare in his nature, but in his final days he came to terms with it.

Other episodes were not so pleasant. Claude caused emotional distress by obtaining a court order demanding that

231

Pablo acknowledge him as a son. The case revived all the hate and worry of the Françoise affair. There was a new flood of embarrassing publicity.

Once at a bullfight, Claude was able to wave at Pablo from a distance, but Pablo showed no interest. Paloma did eventually have one meeting with Pablo at Notre-Dame-de-Vie, but it was brief and chilly. Now the press criticized him for penalizing his children for something their mother had done. This was uncomfortably true.

Jacqueline, who feared all distractions, was more upset by Claude's legal action than Pablo. But it soon blew over. The family lawyer won a ruling against Claude. When Claude was born, the judge said, Pablo had still been married to Olga and could not, therefore, be considered the legal father.

Pablo once again gave full attention to his work. It was not unusual for him to create both a painting and an etching in a single day. Often he worked far into the night, and instead of sleeping late after such an effort as he had in the past, he rose early in order to have another productive day.

Friends marveled at his enthusiasm as much as his energy. He had collected several monoprints by Edgar Degas, and when he showed them to visitors, he said they were the best things Degas had ever done. This opinion may have been due in part to Degas's subject matter—scenes in brothels.

Pablo was focusing more and more attention on erotic themes. Early in 1971, he began a long series of etchings based on the Degas monoprints. They were to keep him occupied until his final days. Many of these prints depicted Degas as an observer in the brothel. The sexual activities he observed left very little to the imagination. Indeed, many critics think that Pablo's sense of the erotic degenerated, in his final months, to the obscene. Jacqueline would not let Pablo show some of the brothel prints to anyone, not even their closest friends.

Nearly every day some city of the world announced the

232

opening of a new Picasso show. The shows close to home, however, gave Pablo the most pleasure. He was most interested in the shows of recent work held at the Palace of the Popes, in Avignon, some hundred miles west of Mougins. Christian and Yvonne Zervos organized the first show in 1970.

The press had a delightful time describing the erotic work hanging in the rooms where the French popes once had lived and held audience. It was a major show, drawing huge crowds from May through October.

Unfortunately, Yvonne Zervos died before the show opened, and Christian Zervos outlived her by only eight months. Here were more stark reminders of mortality. Christian Zervos had been a loyal friend for forty-four years and had spent much of that time cataloguing Picasso's work.

Meanwhile, the Avignon show was such a success that museum officials asked for another Picasso exhibit. Pablo said he would think about it.

Soon after the Avignon show, Pablo, age eighty-nine, joined a political protest. It happened that the Franco regime had condemned six Spaniards to death for working for the independence of the Basque provinces of Spain. The liberal press denounced Franco as a tyrant, and the world declared that the penalty was too severe.

For his part, Pablo ordered cancellation of ceremonies that had been scheduled to unveil his recent gifts to the Barcelona museum. Early in 1971, thanks largely to pressure from the pope, Franco did commute the death sentences to life imprisonment. Pablo shared some of the glory of this victory.

To honor his ninetieth birthday, the French government staged a Picasso show at the Louvre. It was, however, a very modest show, reflecting the conservative government's continued reserve. There were just eight paintings, with nothing that represented his recent work. Although Pablo and

Jacqueline had flown to Paris for the opening of a show of his recent drawings in Galerie Louise Leiris a few months earlier, he did not attend the show at the Louvre.

He even failed to appear as promised in nearby Vallauris, where the town fathers had prepared a birthday celebration. He hated to disappoint the people of Vallauris, but the fact was that public appearances now exhausted him. He needed all his energy for his work.

In his final year, Jacqueline allowed even fewer visitors. Reports varied. Some who came away from Notre-Dame-de-Vie said that Pablo seemed sad and depressed. He looked smaller, as if his body had shrunk. Others said he was the same robust Pablo, full of surprises, good cheer, and laughter. It seems that Pablo, as usual, had many moods, leaving different impressions on different friends.

Early in 1973, he agreed to a second show of recent work at the Palace of the Popes in Avignon. He decided to show 201 paintings, most of them dealing with the erotic scenes that continued to fascinate him.

Planning the new show held most of his attention, but frequent bouts with the flu sometimes forced him to remain in bed all day. Often, when recovering, he would turn on the television and make quick sketches from the fleeting images.

His flu touched off rumors that Pablo was seriously ill, but the doctors were not worried, and Jacqueline assured concerned friends that there was no problem. In March, Pablo returned to his usual full schedule of work.

He was in good health right up until April 7, 1973. He and Jacqueline entertained another couple that evening. Pablo was tired, but he had trouble getting to sleep. It was hard for him to breathe. Early in the morning he began gasping. Jacqueline at once sent for the family doctor, and the doctor immediately sent for a specialist.

By the time the specialist had arrived, Pablo had fallen into a restless sleep. He muttered from time to time as if he were dreaming. Shortly before noon, the muttering stopped. Pablo, age ninety-one, was dead. It was April 8, 1973.

The news bulletin, issued that afternoon, gave as the cause of death a heart attack brought on by a pulmonary edema, or fluid in the lungs. Despite his age, the news came as a shock to the world. There had been little warning. It had seemed to some that the dynamo would never stop, that Pablo Picasso would go on forever.

Jacqueline wanted Pablo buried at Mougins, but a town ordinance would not allow private burials. So Vauvenargues was selected. Pablo had not visited the château for many months. It had never been a permanent home, but he had loved the view of Sainte-Victoire, the mountain that had been Cézanne's obsession.

The burial was as private as Jacqueline could make it. She, her mother, her daughter, Paulo, and Miguel, Pablo's secretary, represented the Picasso household. Jacqueline had invited a small delegation from the Vauvenargues town council, but there were no other outsiders.

Marie-Thérèse Walter, Maya, Claude, and Paloma all tried to attend but were turned away by guards. This was sad. Tragedy was soon to follow.

On the day of the burial, Pablo's grandson, Pablito, swallowed a container of laundry bleach, which caused fatal damage to his intestines. He lingered in a hospital for three months before he died. Reason for the suicide was unclear. The boy apparently took the bleach after hearing his father, Paulo, arguing with his estranged wife over money problems. Later, Paulo's wife stated publicly that she could not have paid for the expensive operations that might have saved Pablito's life. She could not even pay the hospital bills.

Of course, most magazines and newspapers treated the case as another Picasso scandal in a long line of scandals. His death itself had already touched off a series of journalistic excesses.

In obituaries, some writers lauded Pablo in such generous terms that they made him seem superhuman; others, focusing on his sex life and his politics, made him appear as an ogre. Newspapers and magazines tried to outdo each other with photos and long articles spread over several pages. Unfortunately, these articles usually devoted more space to his personal life than to his artistic achievements.

French editors, critical of the "alien" Picasso during his lifetime, now tried to claim him as a product of France. Spanish editors countered by citing Pablo's true heritage.

More serious journals did their best to assess Pablo's art and his influence on other artists. In light of his long career and massive output, this was not an easy job.

The debate over Picasso's huge body of work will continue long after most events of our century are forgotten. On one point, however, most people agree: Pablo Picasso changed the way we see things.

The monetary value of Picasso's work doubled and even tripled soon after his death. A few months before he died, a painting had sold in New York for $280,000. Soon after his death, it was worth close to $1,000,000. His drawings, some selling for $25,000 and more before his death, went to six figures soon after.

With prices soaring ever higher, it was almost impossible to put a value on Pablo's estate. For tax purposes, the figure was eventually set at $312 million. But this underestimated the real value of most of his paintings. Some unofficial estimates said the estate was worth closer to $1 billion.

Who would get it? Pablo Picasso had died without leaving a will. This set off one of the longest, most bitter legal fights the French courts had ever known. It began when his illegitimate children Maya, Claude, and Paloma, less than a month after his death, filed suit demanding a complete inventory of the estate. This was the first in a series of suits and countersuits, court hearings, and challenges that continued for years. The French government, seeking death duties from the estate, eventually entered the legal battle and became a major winner in the contest. The rest of the estate was divided among Jacqueline, Maya, Claude, Paloma, and the estate of Paulo Picasso, who had died of drug and alcohol abuse before his father's estate was settled.

Under a provision of French inheritance tax, the death duties, the government received enough Picassos to fill a warehouse. At last, the French had no choice but to build a Picasso museum. Today, it is one of Paris's major attractions, both for tourists as well as art lovers. It includes Pablo's collection of African masks and works by other artists covered in his bequest.

Tragedy continued to hound Picasso's family. Following Paulo's death in 1974, Marie-Thérèse Walter hanged herself in 1977, and in 1986, Jacqueline Picasso, after saying she could no longer live without Pablo, shot herself.

There were, however, some happy endings. Françoise made her own way as an artist and eventually married Jonas Salk, inventor of the polio vaccine. Paloma, also happily married, has found fame and success in the fashion industry. She is extremely proud of her remarkable father.

BIBLIOGRAPHY

Barr, Alfred H., Jr. *Picasso: Fifty Years of His Art.* New York: Museum of Modern Art, 1946.

Brassaï, Jules Halasz. *Picasso and Co.* New York: Doubleday, 1967.

Cabanne, Pierre. *Picasso: His Life and Times.* Translated by Harold J. Salemson. New York: William Morrow, 1977.

Castleman, Riva. *Prints of the Twentieth Century: A History.* New York: Museum of Modern Art, 1976.

De la Croix, Horst, and Richard G. Tansey. *Gardner's Art Through the Ages,* Vol. II. New York: Harcourt, Brace, Jovanovich, 1986.

Diehl, Gaston. *Picasso.* Translated by Helen C. Slonim. New York: Crown Publishers, 1952.

Duncan, David Douglas. *The Private World of Pablo Picasso.* New York: Ridge Press, 1957.

―――. *Picasso's Picassos.* New York: Harper, 1961.

Elgar, Frank, and Robert Maillard. *Picasso.* Translated by Francis Scarfe. New York: Frederick A. Praeger, 1956.

Gilot, Françoise, and Carlton Lake. *Life with Picasso.* New York: Avon Books, 1964.

Gimcher, Arnold, and Marc Gimcher, eds. *The Sketchbooks of Picasso.* New York: Atlantic Monthly Press, 1986.

Hunt, George P., ed. "Picasso: Special Edition." *Life,* December 27, 1968.

Jardot, Maurice. *Pablo Picasso: Drawings.* New York: Abrams, 1959.

Lake, Carlton, and Robert Maillard, eds. *Dictionary of Modern Painting.* New York: Tudor, 1957.

Los Angeles County Museum of Art. *Picasso: Sixty Years of Graphic Works.* Greenwich, Conn.: New York Graphic Society, 1966.

Penrose, Roland. *Picasso: His Life and Work.* 3d ed. Berkeley: University of California Press, 1981.

―――. *Homage to Picasso.* London: Lund Humphries, 1951.

―――. *Portrait of Picasso.* London: Lund Humphries, 1956.

Spies, Werner. *Sculpture by Picasso, with a Catalogue of the Works.* New York: Abrams, 1971.

Stein, Gertrude. *Autobiography of Alice B. Toklas.* Harmondsworth: Penguin Books, 1970.

―――. *Everybody's Autobiography.* New York: Random House, 1937.

INDEX

abstract art, 184, 212
Accordionist, 76
Acrobat Family with Monkey, 50
Actor, The, 50
Afternoon of a Faun, 220
American Artists' Congress (1937),
  138
Animal Head, 182
Antigone (Sophocles), 108
antique period, 102–10
Apollinaire, Guillaume, 47, 51, 54,
  77, 84, 99–100, 121–22, 153
aquatint, 223
Aragon, Louis, 194
Arnera (linoleum craftsman), 215
Arte Joven (Young Art), 33–34
Arts, 109
Autobiography of Alice B. Toklas,
  The (Stein), 122

Baboon with Young, 203
Ballets Russes, 90, 97, 106, 109,
  220
Barcelona School of Fine Arts (La
  Lonja; Stock Market), 14, 17, 23
Barr, Alfred J., Jr., 226
Bathsheba (Rembrandt), 217
Beaumont, Count Cyril, 109
Bernhardt, Sarah, 162
Blind Man, 117
blue period, 37–41, 42, 48, 51, 64,
  69, 80, 105, 117, 227
Braque, Georges, 73–74, 81, 83, 86,
  87, 100, 105, 106, 122, 200, 201,
  214, 222
  Picasso's collaboration with,
    60–61, 64, 66–69, 71–72,
    75–76, 78, 107, 162–63, 170,
    188

Brassaï, Jules, 140–41
Breker, Arno, 150–51
brothel prints, 232–33
Bull's Head, 153
Burial of Casagemas, The, 37
Burial of Count Orgaz (El Greco), 19, 37
Busquets, Xavier, 218

Cahiers d'Art (Art Notebooks), 112
Can Can, 31
Capa, Robert, 157
Cardona, Josep, 24
Carré, Louis, 161
Casagemas, Carlos, 25, 27, 28, 30, 31, 32, 33, 45
    suicide of, 32, 34, 37, 40
Casas, Ramon, 35
Cassou, Jean, 177–78
Cézanne, Paul, 35, 64, 67–68, 101, 150, 214, 235
    influence on Picasso of, 31, 40, 59, 61, 69
    see also cubism, Cézannesque
Charnel House, The, 161
Choirboy, The, 16
classicism, 94, 101, 102, 227
Clouzot, Henri-Georges, 202–3
Cocteau, Jean, 89, 95, 100, 107, 109, 150–51, 157, 187, 191, 200, 205, 222
    theater and, 89–97, 108
Colegio San Rafaelo, 5
collaborators, 148–49, 151
Colle, Pierre, 150
College of Architecture, 218
Communism, 127–28, 130, 157–58, 169, 206, 213
Communist party, Spanish:
    art as viewed by, 160, 169, 177, 184
    Picasso's membership in, 155–61, 206, 225
Compote Bowl and Glass, 80

Congress of Intellectuals for Peace (1948), 178–79
Cooper, Gary, 200
Cranach, Lucas, 171–72
Crommelinck, Aldo and Pietro, 221, 223, 228
Cuadro flamenco, 106–7, 108
Cuba, Antonio, 14, 15
cubism, 62–72, 74–76, 83, 84, 86, 99, 101, 105, 112, 160, 188
    analytic, 76
    Cézannesque, 76
    costume construction—style of, 94
    enemies of, 96–97, 106
    reconstruction style of, 68, 86
    symbolic, 134
    synthetic, 76, 78, 80, 84, 107
cutouts, 193, 217
Cuttoli, Marie, 167

dadaism, 101, 103, 106
Dalí, Salvador, 112, 127
Dance, 110, 112
David and Bathsheba (Cranach), 171–72
Debussy, Claude, 90
de Falla, Manuel, 102
Degas, Edgar, 31, 232
de Gaulle, Charles, 225
Degrain, Antonio Muñoz, 3–4, 5, 18–19
Delacroix, Eugène, 31, 197–99
Demoiselles d'Avignon, Les (The Young Ladies of Avignon), 62–67, 109–10
Diaghilev, Serge, 90–92, 94–97, 102, 104, 106–7, 109
Dor de la Souchère, Ramuald, 168, 174–75, 178, 199
Douglas, David Duncan, 209
"dove" poster, 180–81
Dream and Lie of Franco, 132, 133
Dubois, André-Louis, 149

241

El Greco, 11, 19, 33, 37
Éluard, Marie Benz "Nush," 128,
   152, 155, 170, 178
Éluard, Paul, 127, 129, 131, 137,
   146, 170, 187, 189, 220
   as communist, 127–28, 149,
      155, 157–58, 169, 178, 184
etchings, 162, 178, 180, 182, 201,
   215, 221, 223
Etruscan art, 104

Fall of Icarus, The, see UNESCO
   painting
fascism, 130, 135, 138, 231
fauves, 60–61, 67, 84–85
Faÿ, Bernard, 158
First Communion, 16
Flayed Head, 153
Flower Woman, The, 165–66
found objects, 101, 122, 182, 188,
   191
Four Cats, 24–25, 27, 58, 231
Four Little Girls, 189
Franco, Francisco, 130–32, 134, 140,
   141, 205, 217–18, 225, 233
Frugal Repast, The, 38
futurists, 94

Galerie Louise Leiris, 210, 213, 223,
   234
Galerie Paul Guillaume, 98
García Lorca, Federico, 131, 192
Garoupe, La, 202
Gauguin, Paul, 31, 35, 40, 64
Germaine (model), 32, 33, 34, 45
gestapo, 149, 154, 156
Gilot, Françoise, 155, 157, 160–61,
   164, 165, 166, 167–75, 179,
   181–82, 183, 184, 186–93,
   199–200, 201, 224, 237
Girl Singing, 85
González, Julio, 121–22, 153
Gouel, Eva, 78–81, 83, 86–89, 188

Goya, Francisco de, 11, 19
Grand Palais, 28, 226
Greek art, influence of, 59, 102, 104,
   176, 222
Gris, Juan, 106–7
Guernica, 132–37, 140, 150, 161,
   185, 222, 226
Guitar, 231

Harlequin, 88, 89
Harlequin Family, 117
Hemingway, Ernest, 54, 157
Hitler, Adolf, 130, 140, 144, 147,
   150
Humbert, Marcelle, *see* Gouel, Eva
Hymn for the Dead (Reverdy), 164

Icarus (Lifar), 220–21
impressionists, 5, 13–14, 82, 98
Inez, 137, 152, 155, 157, 170, 201
Ingres, Jean, 31, 104
Instituto da Guarda, 8

Jacob, Max, 36, 39, 43–44, 45, 47,
   48, 54, 55, 73–76, 81, 90, 100,
   105, 151, 154

Kahnweiler, Daniel-Henry, 64–66,
   68–70, 72, 74–75, 80–81, 85, 86,
   87, 104, 105, 106, 111, 122, 151,
   154, 158, 159–60, 161, 179, 180,
   186, 187, 197, 200, 209, 213
Keller-Shchukine, Irene, 194–195
Khoklova, Olga, *see* Picasso, Olga
   Khoklova
Kootz, Samuel, 180
Korean War, 184–85

Lacourière, Roger, 118
Lake, Carlton, 224
Last Moments, 28
Le Corbusier, 213
Leiris, Louise, 151, 187, 200, 209, 210

Leiris, Michel, 122, 151, 187, 200, 209, 210
Lettres Françaises, Les, 158, 190
Leymarie, Jean, 226, 228
Lifar, Serge, 220–21
Life, 141, 157
linoleum-block prints, 215–17
lithography, 162–67, 171, 180, 199, 201, 215
"logbook," 228
Lonja, La, 14, 17, 23
Louvre, 31, 71, 77, 212, 233–34
Lunchcon on the Grass (Manet), 216–17
Luncheon on the Grass (Picasso), 216–17

Maar, Dora, 128–32, 135, 137–38, 141–46, 148, 151, 152, 153–56, 160–61, 167, 170, 220
Madrid General Fine Arts Exhibition (1897), 16
Maison de la Pensée Française, 179
Ma Jolie, 79
Malraux, André, 225–26
Manach, Pedro, 31, 32, 33, 35, 36, 37, 39, 40, 43
Manet, Édouard, 31, 216–17
Man with Guitar, 76
Man with the Sheep, 157, 185, 203
Markus, Louis, 78
masks, 17, 59, 60, 70, 203, 237
Massacre in Korea, 185
"maternities," 40, 105
Matisse, Henri, 54, 59, 60, 64, 66, 82, 92, 98, 101, 105, 139–40, 150, 170, 193, 197, 199, 204, 213, 214
Meninas, Las (Maids of Honor) (Velásquez), 11, 207–9
Meninas, Las (Picasso), 207–11
Milliner's Workshop, The, 112, 178
Minotaure, 123

Model and Surrealist Sculpture, 120
modern art, 31, 54, 55, 82, 84, 97, 103, 106, 159
Modigliani, Amedeo, 92
Moulin de la Galette, Le, 31, 32
Mourlot, Fernand, 162–67, 171, 176, 179, 180, 191, 197
Museo Picasso, 14, 211, 222, 231
Museum of Modern Art, 142, 169, 206, 226, 231
Mussolini, Benito, 130
My Life with Picasso (Gilot), 224
Mystère Picasso, Le (Clouzot), 202–3

Nazis, 147–50, 156, 184
Neoclassicism, 31
Neruda, Pablo, 179
Night Fishing at Antibes, 142–44, 143
nonobjective art, 169–70, 179, 184
Nude with a Musician, 178

Oedipus Rex (Sophocles), 174
O'Keeffe, Georgia, 77
Old Guitar Player, 44
Olivier, Fernande, 47–50, 51, 54, 55, 57, 58–60, 64, 66–71, 75, 78–80, 122–24, 200–201, 222

Pablo's Gang, 39, 73
Palace of the Popes, 233, 234
Pallarés y Grau, Manuel, 15–23, 25, 28, 31, 34, 39, 69
Parade, 92–98
Paris Opera, 220
Parmelin, Hélène, see Pignon, Hélène Parmelin
Paulhan, Jean, 170
Petit Palais, 137, 226, 227
Philadelphia Academy of Fine Arts, 181
Photo Session Gallery, 76–77, 82

Picasso, Claude (son), 172, 174, 181, 184, 188, 189, 193, 195, 201, 224, 231–32, 235, 236–37

Picasso, Jacqueline Roque (second wife), 193–200, 202–3, 204, 205, 209, 210, 211, 214, 216, 219–20, 221, 226, 231–37

Picasso, María de la Concepción "Maya" (daughter), 125, 129, 130, 132, 140, 141, 144–45, 151, 156, 172, 173, 188, 192, 195, 201, 235, 236–37

Picasso, Olga Khoklova (first wife), 95–102, 104–6, 107, 108–9, 111–16, 119, 122, 124–25, 126, 128, 130, 151, 173–74, 177, 199, 200, 232

Picasso, Pablito (grandson), 235

Picasso, Pablo:
    birth of, 1–2
    death of, 234–35
    education of, 2, 5–6, 8–9, 14–15, 16–20, 23
    physical appearance of, 3, 42, 98
    political involvement of, 128, 130–38, 236
    women and, 39, 45, 106, 114, 119–21, 151, 160, 189–90, 193, 236

Picasso, Paloma (daughter), 181, 184, 188, 189, 191, 193, 195, 201, 224, 232, 235, 236–37

Picasso, Paulo (Paul) (son), 106, 107–8, 109, 114, 124, 151, 171, 173, 188–89, 201, 219, 235, 237

Picasso: Portraits and Souvenirs (Sabartés), 145

Picasso y Lopez, Doña María (mother), 1, 2, 8, 43, 81, 108, 138, 141, 142, 230

Pignon, Édouard, 189, 195, 209, 210, 223

Pignon, Hélène Parmelin, 189, 195, 209, 210, 222, 228

poetry, of Picasso, 126–27, 129

Pompeii, 104

Portrait of a Painter, After El Greco, 184

postimpressionists, 31, 82

pottery, 176–78

Poussin, Nicolas, 156

Pozner, Vladimir, 204

Prado Museum, 11, 19, 131

Pregnant Woman, 182, 203

Prévert, Jacques, 205

primitive art, 54, 59–61, 77, 122, 218

Provincial Exhibition at Málaga, 16

Pulcinella, 104

Ramié, Georges, 168, 176–77, 179, 181, 182, 191, 195, 206

Ramié, Suzanne, 168, 176–77, 179, 181, 182, 191, 195

Rape of the Sabine Woman, The, 221–22

Ravel, Maurice, 90

reduction method, 215

Rembrandt, 217, 224, 229

Renoir, Claude, 202

Renoir, Pierre-Auguste, 35, 150

Reservoir at Horta, 69

Reverdy, Pierre, 164

Roman art, 102, 104, 222

Romanticism, 31

Romeu, Père, 24

Roque, Catharine, 194, 201, 235

Rosenberg, Léonce, 100, 104, 106, 118, 154

Rosenberg, Paul, 100, 102, 104, 117, 118, 154

rose period, 48–57, 69, 80, 109, 117, 227

Rouquette, Jean-Maurice, 231

Rubens, Peter Paul, 19

Rubinstein, Arthur, 205
Ruiz Blasco, Don José (father),
    1–11, 13–20, 41, 43, 58, 81, 90,
    135, 172
Ruiz Blasco, Pablo (uncle), 3
Ruiz Blasco, Salvador (uncle), 1, 2,
    10, 18, 19, 20, 33, 41
Ruiz Picasso, Lola (sister), 3–4, 6, 8,
    11, 26, 81
Ruiz Picasso, María de la
    Concepción (sister), 6, 8, 10
Russia, market for Picassos in, 66
Russian Revolution, 194

Sabartés, Jaime, 25, 39, 42–43,
    44–45, 125–27, 129–30, 137,
    140–45, 155, 160, 170, 200, 202,
    205, 209, 217–18, 222, 230
Saint Severin, 214
Sala Parés, 26, 34, 35
Salk, Jonas, 237
Salles, George, 211, 212
Salmon, André, 47
Salome, 55, 56
Salon d'Automne, 158–59
San Fernando Academy, 18, 116
San Telmo School of Arts and
    Crafts, 3
Satie, Erik, 90–94, 97, 109
Schilperoort, Tom, 55
Science and Charity, 16
sculpture, 26, 86, 118–22, 146, 171,
    176, 182
    work of Picasso in, 152–53,
    217, 227
Seated Nude, 50
Self-Portrait with Wig, 14
Seventy-Fifth Anniversary Picasso
    Exhibition, 206
She-Goat, 182, 203
Silver Medal of French Gratitude,
    178
Skira, Albert, 117, 123

Song of the Rivers (Pozner), 204
Soto, Mateo de, 39
Sputnik, 211
Stalin, Joseph, 190–91, 206
Stein, Allen, 57
Stein, Gertrude, 51–61, 63, 64, 66,
    71, 83, 87, 90, 99, 105, 108, 122,
    154, 158, 160, 170, 194
Stein, Leo, 52–54, 57, 71
Stein, Michael, 52
Stieglitz, Alfred, 77, 82–83
Stiff Shirts, 31
Still Life Beneath the Lamp, 215
Still Life with Chair Caning, 80
Still Life with Oranges, 178
Still Life with Sheep, 145
Stock Market, 14
Stravinsky, Igor, 90, 94, 104
surrealism, 112

Tate Gallery, 210
television, 221
temple of peace, 185–86
theater, modern art in, 18, 90–97,
    102, 108, 221
Third Municipal Exposition of Fine
    Arts, 16
Three-Cornered Hat, The, 102
Three Dutch Girls, 85
Three Musicians, 107
Titian, 19
Toklas, Alice B., 71, 99, 158, 160
Toreador on Horseback, 6
To the Spanish Republicans Who
    Died for France, 161
Toulouse-Lautrec, Henri de, 31,
    32
Train Bleu, Le, 109
Triumph of Pan (Poussin), 156

Uhde, Wilhelm, 51, 64, 72, 106
UNESCO painting, 207, 210,
    211–13, 221

245

United States, modern art in, 82–83, 116

Universal Exposition (1900), 28

Van Dyck, Sir Anthony, 19
van Gogh, Vincent, 31, 36–37, 67
Velázquez, Diego, 11, 19, 207–9
Vichy France, 148–49, 158
Vie, La (Life), 45
Visage (Face), 115
Vlaminck, Maurice de, 148–49
Vollard, Ambroise, 34–36, 37, 40, 47, 52, 57, 58, 62, 64, 72, 117–18, 129, 142
Vollard Suite, 118, 193, 222

Walter, Marie-Thérèse, 114–16, 119–21, 122, 124–25, 128–30, 132, 138, 140, 141, 144–46, 151, 153–54, 156–57, 167, 173, 188, 201, 235, 237

War and Peace, 192
Weill, Berthe, 31, 43
Woman Beneath the Lamp, 215
Woman Dressing Her Hair, 146
Woman in an Armchair, 145
Woman with a Guitar, 79
Woman with Baby Carriage, 188
Women of Algiers (Delacroix), 197
Women of Algiers (Picasso), 197–99
World War I, 85–99
World War II, 130–56

Young Girl in White Near a Window, 26
Young Ladies along the Seine, After Courbet, 184

Zervos, Christian, 112, 131, 137, 146, 201, 233
Zervos, Yvonne, 233
Zurbarán, Francisco de, 11, 19